STORIES BY GERALD M. SIEGEL

YOU SHOULDA
BEEN THERE

Jerry Siegel

BROOKLYN · IOWA · NORTH DAKOTA · KANSAS · ISRAEL · MINNESOTA

The following stories were published previously in The American Jewish World: "Mrs. Siegel's Christmas Lights" (also in Identity and Jewish Digest); "Mrs. Siegel at Home" (also in Der Bay); "North Side Memories"; "A Cantor for All Seasons" (also in Modern Liturgy and the Minnesota Daily); "A Sign upon Your Hands" (also in Church Musician Today); "Hillel and Shammai: A Modern Spin on an Old Story" (also in CJ: Voices of Conservative Judaism); "How Many Candles"; "Elana's Magic Dreidle"; "Passover Preparations"; "Finding the Afikomen"; "Pass the Bread, Please"; "More Maror"; "Elijah's Cup"; "Passover Reflections" (also in Horizons); "Anna's Recollections" (also in Welcome to Israel); "The Road to Chelm"; "Sign of the Covenant"; "This Isn't Netflix" (also in Pakn Treger); "A Suit with Two Pairs of Pants" (also in Western Cleaners and Launderers).

The following stories were published previously in Identity:" Louis and Me" (published as "Sam and Me") (also in Green's Magazine; Jewish Spectator; Aim, as "The Magic Circle"); "Auspicious Beginning" (also in Green's Magazine); "You Shoulda Been There: An intergenerational Guide for Children Whose Parents Grew Up in New York" (also in ORT Reporter); "Mr. Mogol"; "The Invisible Costume"; "Jelly Bread Up, Jelly Bread Down" (also in the Minnesota Daily); "Going Kosher" (also in Amit).

The following stories were published previously in CJ: Voices of Conservative Judaism: "The Men Are Coming"; "Freedom Seder" (also in Midstream).

The following stories were published previously in Congress Monthly: "Choir of the Whole" (also in Church Musician Today); "Soil from Israel"; "The Road to Masada"; "Perpetual Care"; "Jurisdictional Dispute"; "In Search of a Friday-Night Challah."

The following stories were published previously in Welcome to Israel: "Israel through the Eyes of a Washing Machine" (also in Western Cleaners and Launderers); "Kfar Menachem."

"Sticks and Stones" was published previously in Green's Magazine and in the Minneapolis Tribune; "Across the Ocean to Iowa," and "A Most Fragile Friendship" were published in Response; "Mr. Mayberg Reads Torah," in Reconstructionist; "Purim Shpiel," in Jewish Spectator.

All of the previously published stories were edited for this volume.

Cover design by Cathy Spengler; book design and production by Corey Sevett, Artisan Creative Computer Services.

Preface

I joined the faculty of the Department of Speech, Language, and Hearing Sciences at the University of Minnesota in the fall of 1961. In 1974 I came across *Identity,* a small literary magazine published by the Minneapolis Jewish Community Center. On impulse, I submitted "Mrs. Siegel's Christmas Lights," based on a recent visit to my mother in Brooklyn, New York. It was included in the November issue of *Identity.* From then on, until the magazine ceased in the mid-1980s, there was hardly an issue that didn't contain one of my stories, and creative writing became an indispensible part of my life. My stories have appeared in such diverse places as *Western Cleaners and Launderers, Handball Magazine, Chicken Soup for Nurses, Sun Country In-Flight Magazine, Church Musician Today,* and *Modern Liturgy,* as well as such Jewish publications as *Midstream, Congress Monthly, ORT Reporter, Jewish Digest,* and *CJ: Voices of Conservative Judaism.*

Writing for publication is both deflating and exhilarating. "Louis and Me" was rejected by twenty-one magazines until it was accepted by *Jewish Currents, Jewish Spectator,* and *Aim. Midstream* held "Headlines" for six years before it finally appeared, and "Shabbos in Brooklyn" has been in press with *Jewish Currents* since 2002. I sent "Israel through the Eyes of a Washing Machine" to *Western Cleaners and Launderers,* a trade magazine, never expecting it would be accepted. Some months later I received a letter from Wakefield Publishing Company that looked like junk mail, and I tossed it. Later that day I raced home to search through the trash. Sure enough, it contained a check and a copy of the article. I submitted "My Brief Career as a Medical Student" to a contest sponsored by *Sun Country In-Flight Magazine* in April of 2006. I heard nothing from them and assumed they had passed on it. In December, Jane Falk, someone I didn't know, called from California to tell me how much she had enjoyed it. Through her kindness I learned that it had indeed been published, and that I was owed the free airline ticket promised to winning entries.

The stories in this book are situated in Brooklyn, Iowa, North Dakota, Kansas, Minnesota, Israel, and fictional lands of the imagination. They are written with affection for the places and the people in them. They touch on themes of family, loss, celebration, and community. Some have been previously published. All have been edited and revised for this volume.

Phil Freshman edited the first four stories. Laura Silver provided professional editing for the entire book. The cover was designed with the patient artistry of Cathy Spengler. The photograph on the cover is of me, my brother, Joel, and my cousin Larry Field. The 79th Street station was our stop on the BMT line, just blocks from home. Corey Sevett designed the interior of the book.

I am grateful to my wife, Eileen, whose encouragement persuaded me it is time to bring my stories into book form. I hope that my children and grandchildren will find enough family lore in these pages to understand some of our eccentricities, and to feel rewarded. I dearly wish our daughter, Karen, had been here to participate in the pleasure of seeing this work in print.

Gerald M. Siegel, 2012

Contents

Here and There,
Then and Now

Headlines

THE TROLLEY IS GONE along New Utrecht Avenue, the one that used to take us to Coney Island, but the elevated train still stops at New Utrecht and Seventy-Ninth Street, just a block from New Utrecht High School on one side, and a block and a half from my former home on the other.

Once a year I return to New York to visit my brother and mother and uncles and aunts and cousins and in-laws. They're still there, the most adventuresome having moved to Long Island. My father and my wife's father died years ago. Our mothers and the aunts and uncles are in their seventies. They have creaky bodies and arthritis. The women have joined the developing society of widows. Last year, it was Esther Schneider's husband. Last month, Uncle Joe. The women, alone, cling to each other more than to their children. The old folks with their rickety Medicared bodies are living according to an orderly and sensible plan. They buried their parents. They raised their children and ushered them into marriage. They became grandparents and loved their grandchildren. They learned to endure one another. As they've aged, they've continued to care for, as well as to blame, one another, and to live for their children and grandchildren as much as for themselves.

There is pain and disappointment in growing old, but the chaos is in the next generation. The children and the grandchildren are not living according to an orderly and sensible plan. Marriages are faltering after decades. Children are estranged from their parents. Jewish children are marrying Italians, and blacks, and Asians and are inviting their parents and grandparents to the ceremony—*in church*. The daughters are raising careers rather than children. The old folks yearn for a bris, or a naming ceremony, or a bar or bat mitzvah to sustain them. Instead, they have the specter of their children's lives crumbling, of families torn apart, of a daughter-in-law or a son-in-law who for years was a child to them suddenly wrenched out of the family to become a stranger again. The chaos is in the younger generation, but the old folks are suffering the dislocation. The physical and emotional shelter they expected at the end of a long road will not be there for them.

When I return to New York each year my brother meets me at the airport and I spend the night with him. That's when I get to see how tall my young nephew has grown; he will be visiting my brother for the weekend. Then I go to my mother's apartment. One evening the relatives will come, those who are able, and congregate in her living room to ask about my family and to talk about theirs. They are a boisterous group who come alive during an argument. Their speech is laced with superlatives, and there is no topic unworthy of ferocious debate.

My mother-in-law lives only a few stations away on the B train. The train cars are newer than I recall but more decayed and covered with graffiti. My anxiety about that visit begins mounting as soon as I set out to visit her. I do not know if my brother-in-law will greet me warmly or, more likely, will be sullen and angry as he has been for the past twenty-six years since we left New York, and he began his long siege of mental illness in and out of institutions, shock treatments, therapies, and medications. He has remained incredibly handsome, his face unlined, his hair still a thick, dark auburn. Once he was my boyhood friend but his mind is haunted and he protects himself from the pain in his world by anger and solitude. My visits are unsettling, an intrusion, but I feel compelled to make this painful yearly pilgrimage to visit him and my mother-in-law.

I must also stop at Uncle Meyer's grocery store. It is only his shadow that will appear at my mother's soiree, and a dozing shadow at that. Uncle Meyer assumes full profile at his counter, by his cash register, wearing his white apron, exchanging barbs with the old customers and hangers-on who have made a social-service center of the tiny grocery.

New York is a city of theaters, museums, parks, and concerts, but at most I will have a few hours to walk the busy, crowded, dense streets, past the New York Times Building where I worked as a copy boy for Reuters, along the Eighth Avenue strip that has become a human deprave-yard, into the excitement of the Theater District, and perhaps along Fifth Avenue, toward the park. I would like to do more, but my mother's old friend Rachel is coming to see me that afternoon, and so is my Aunt Ann, and I've barely touched the pea soup my mother made especially for me, or talked solemnly about my brother's separation from his wife.

Manhattan, Brooklyn, Seventy-Seventh Street, relatives, the noisy subway, the splendor of the Brooklyn Bridge, the pulsing excitement of a New York street, the pulse of fear when a stranger approaches, the premonition of violence and the flash of memories tender and tearful—it is too much to record. There are stories everywhere, but they are too many and too jumbled to sort and tell. Memories and impressions combine into a collage of headlines and short shorts, melding finally into some sort of order. It has been a month since my last visit, and that's what I've preserved, headlines and short shorts.

MAYOR KOCH REQUESTS 10,000 BULLET-PROOF VESTS FOR CITY'S FINEST.

ROLLER DISCO FIRE BOMBED. SUSPECT IN CUSTODY.

SIEGEL RETURNS. G. Siegel returns to Brooklyn, where he is violently assaulted by relatives, in-laws, and memories.

KNICKS WIN CRUCIAL GAME IN PLAYOFF QUEST.

HEIRLOOM SAVED. Mrs. N. Siegel, living alone at 1774 Seventy-Seventh Street, plunged into the Goldstein apartment just as the wooden chopping bowl belonging to the deceased Mrs. Goldstein was about to be discarded. Authorities have indicated that the scratches and impressions along the interior surface of the bowl may be an obscure code. One message has been tentatively decoded. It appears to be Mrs. Goldstein's recipe for gefilte fish.

TRAGEDY STRIKES GROCERY STORE. Uncle Meyer's wooden pickle barrel has broken beyond repair, spewing forth dozens of hapless pickles. Survivors have been transferred to a new, plastic barrel.

POLICE IN BULLET-PROOF VESTS WARD OFF ANGRY MOB GATHERED TO PROTEST NEW, PLASTIC PICKLE BARREL.

PICKLES GROW WEAK AND LISTLESS.

MRS. SIEGEL TO THE RESCUE AGAIN. This remarkable woman has done it again. She saved the chicken soup by placing herself boldly in front of the boiling cauldron just as her sister was about to add still another pinch of salt.

SOLUTION PRESENTED FOR PICKLE PROBLEM. Under heavy pressure from the community, Uncle Meyer has negotiated a solution to the pickle-barrel predicament. He has retained the plastic barrel but has removed the old pickles. The barrel is now stocked with … plastic pickles.

ALL IS WELL IN NEW YORK.

Mrs. Siegel's Christmas Lights

I WAS IN NEW YORK visiting my mother and we were hurrying home from a shopping excursion, racing to catch a bus. Home was a street in Brooklyn where my mother had lived in the same four-family house for the better part of thirty-nine years, and where I had spent my childhood before getting married and then moving to the Midwest. As far back as I can remember, the landlord had been Mr. Reiff. The other tenants were the Goldsteins, Tannenbaums, and, downstairs in the rear, the Siegels. None of these names went with Christmas lights. In the adjacent house and across the street and farther down the block were the Christmas lights. There was a symmetry on my Brooklyn street: Italian Catholics lived in one three- or four-family building, Jews in another. Side by side, but rarely together.

On the eve of the biblical exodus, when the Israelites were finally rescued from slavery in Egypt, the Jewish homes were marked by an X in lamb's blood as a sign that these houses were to be "passed over" when the last of the plagues, the destruction of the firstborn, was executed against the Egyptians. On my Brooklyn street during Christmas, the Jewish homes were again marked, not with a paschal X, but with darkness. As Christmas approached, the other houses were bathed in lights: bright, colored, blinking lights, pastoral scenes, brightly lit manger scenes, Santa Clauses beckoning (even to Jewish children?), angels ascending and descending, stars and sleighs, and all manner of brilliantly colored and radiant shapes and forms. That was in the other houses. The Jewish houses were dark. The markings were clear and unambiguous. Santa Claus never made a mistake. He never showed his face at my window. Christmas is one of the times that Jews in America know who they are and who they are not.

Times change. People age. They grow fatter or thinner. Hair disappears from one place and crops up in another. People grow old. They look and sound different. Neighborhoods also change. The old people move. New people arrive. The neighborhood develops a new personality. The houses look a little different. The street comes to smell a little different.

That's what happened on my mother's street. A new wave of immigrants took over. Almost all of the Jews moved out. The shop signs on the avenue that had been written in Yiddish all vanished. The Jewish bakery became a mortuary. Izzy's candy store turned into a convenience store, owned by Vietnamese. The market, with its fresh fruit, live fish, kosher meats, and mouthwatering delicatessen became Local Lodge 108 of the Brotherhood of the Moose. Our landlord, Mr. Reiff, died and the new owner, an Italian, wanted my mother's apartment for himself. My mother moved from downstairs-rear to upstairs-front, but the new apartment was almost indistinguishable from the old. Even the cracks in the plaster seemed to be in the same places. Soon she was the only Jewish tenant left. My mother found herself living for the first time in a house with Italians.

During Christmas my mother's new apartment looked out on a street where all the houses were now decorated with lights. Up and down the street were the signs of the season. But upstairs-front, where Mrs. Siegel lives, the window facing the street was framed in darkness. Not a wink; not a flash; not a glimmer. The new landlord, Mr. Delvecchio, just recently arrived from Italy, pleaded with her. For him, the house is a symbol of his pride, his place in the community, and that dark window is a reproach.

"Please Mrs. Siegel, let me put some lights around your window. They're not really *in* your house, see? Just on the outside. I'll put them up, and I'll take them down, and I'll deduct the electricity from your rent bill. It's for my kids, my family. Understand? It's not your lights. All you have to do is just plug them in when it gets dark. OK, Mrs. Siegel?"

What should she do? Could my mother, now an elderly Jewish woman, have Christmas lights on her window? Inside, outside—it was her window and Christmas is surely not her holiday.

We were hurrying home from our shopping spree, racing to catch the bus, and my mother was impatient with me for dawdling.

"Hurry up," she said. "It is getting late."

Where did she get this sudden burst of energy to run after a bus? "What's the hurry?" I asked. "There will be another bus if we miss this one."

"You don't understand," she said. "It's getting dark. Look! All the houses have their Christmas lights on. You can see them a mile away."

It was true, Christmas decorations flickered to life in the houses up and down the block. Once, my mother might have had a rueful comment about gentiles and their Christmas. But now she was out of breath from hurrying home.

"If you are going to do something," she said, "it should be done right. Why should ours be the last house? A man has his dreams. A gentile man has feelings."

Times change. Neighborhoods change. And this new immigrant, this Italian man, my mother's new landlord, he has pride too. And so we were rushing home—to plug in Mr. Delvecchio's Christmas lights.

Mrs. Siegel, at Home

MRS. SIEGEL NO LONGER resides at 1774 Seventy-Seventh Street where I lived until I was married, just a week after my twenty-first birthday. There my brother, Joel, was born in 1938, when I was six, and there we sat shivah for my father, in 1966.

Cars were scarce and children played games on the sidewalks and in the streets. Peddlers hawked their wares in alleyways, aiming their imprecations at second-floor windows, rewarded when a house-wife's head emerged. Sometimes a fiddler would appear in the alley and a few pennies, tightly wrapped in a piece of newspaper, would be tossed from the window. Mike, the milkman, made his deliveries from a horse-drawn cart, as did the iceman. Neighbors occasionally shouted from open windows to catch up on the news, or to remonstrate with their children.

Just about all of the daily necessities could be found within easy walking distance of my home: a market, delicatessen, bakery, cleaner's, corner candy store—with its supply of newspapers, magazines, and comic books, as well as a soda fountain—a barbershop, shoemaker, paint shop, hardware store, butcher shops (kosher and non-kosher), and Italian and Jewish greengrocers. Just a bit farther along, there was a movie theater. Shopping was done on foot, often by mothers pushing baby carriages whose infant passengers were surrounded by groceries. My mother reported that I was not an attractive baby. On one outing, a neighbor stopped, peered at me in the baby carriage, and commented, "My, what a lovely . . . blanket."

Growing up, I was surrounded by my mother's family. My father's parents died when I was very young and I have virtually no memories of them. My maternal grandparents were two blocks away. Uncle Abe moved back with them when he returned from the navy and stayed until he finally married, at the advanced age of thirty-five. When Grandpa died, my grandmother took an apartment in 1772 Seventy-Seventh Street, just across the stoop from us. Uncle Abe and his infant son joined her after his young wife died of cancer. My mother's sister, Aunt Esther, was a block away, and my cousin Larry, Esther's son, ate lunch at my house almost every day. Grandpa's sister, Tante Chaika, and Uncle Ben (her second spouse; his third, but not last) also lived in walking distance. We were beneficiaries of the competition between her and my grandmother over gefilte fish, borscht, and all manner of baked goods. Only Uncle Meyer, my mother's brother, lived more than a few blocks away, but his Pontiac was parked near our house several times each week. My father's brothers and sisters were scattered over Brooklyn, but my mother's clan hung close.

In the early years, all of the tenants in the building were Jewish, at most two generations removed from Eastern Europe. Later, the building was sold to Mr. Delvecchio, an immigrant from Italy. The new landlord, like Mr. Reiff before him, was loathe to spend on heat or electricity, but my mother stayed on, reluctant to move, even as the remaining Jewish families abandoned the neighborhood.

I knew the new landlord only from the annual visits I made from Minnesota. Mr. Delvecchio had two children, a boy and a girl who played on the same stoop that had been my playground, and were just as reluctant to hear their mother calling them inside ("Jiii-m-eeey! Aaa-g-nes!"). He invariably told me what a fine woman my mother was, even as he continued to be stingy with heat, didn't paint at the appointed time, and was slow to make repairs.

The boy, Jimmy, caused trouble. He stole money from my mother's apartment. She reported it to his father, but took no other action. She didn't want unpleasantness. As my mother grew more frail, my aunt and my brother tried to persuade her to move. The steps were too steep. The apartment was cold in winter. Most of the people she knew were long gone. Shopping required a schlep because the Jewish stores and shops were mostly gone, too. Still she stayed on, practically the last "remnant of Israel" in the neighborhood.

My mother was seventy-seven years old and had lived at 1774 Seventy-Seventh Street for fifty years when Mr. Delvecchio, whose Christmas lights she dutifully plugged in, informed her that she had to move. His daughter was to be married, and he wanted the apartment for her. Upstairs-rear, where Mr. and Mrs. Goldstein had lived for decades, was now occupied by a young couple with a baby. The landlord didn't approach them. My mother's apartment was airier, brighter, he said. More to the point, it was still rent-controlled, a holdover from World War II. The landlord could not raise the rent above a modest percentage each year. My mother knew this, and she regularly gave him some money "under the table," but he wanted more.

The thought of moving at her age was daunting. After so many years, how could he do this to her? Her hurt and anger energized her. She would not meekly pack up and go. She would fight. She took the train to Brooklyn's city hall. She climbed stairs. She walked long corridors. She found the office of her city councilman. He sent her to the office of rent controls. They sent her to the office of senior affairs. In the end, she was given a document stipulating that she could not be evicted. She showed the landlord the document. He turned red and said it had been a misunderstanding. He hadn't really meant for her to move. He would evict the young family instead.

My mother had won, but she could no longer live in the same building with that landlord, and she would not be responsible for sending two young people and a baby out into the street. An apartment opened up on Bay Parkway. Her childhood friend Esther Schneider lived in the building, and it would be close to my aunt Esther's place. There were two elevators and heat—blessed heat—throughout the winter. It would be a little smaller and a little more expensive than Seventy-Seventh Street, but she could manage.

Having roused herself to confront the landlord, to enlist city hall, and to find a new place to live, my mother was depleted. She lay down on the couch while all around her my brother, Joel, and his wife, Ann, and other relatives packed the dishes, the supplies of toilet paper, my father's foot powder (still in the medicine cabinet, twenty years past his death), the pictures, the souvenirs—and moved it all to Bay Parkway. The last thing to go was the couch, where my mother lay until the last moment. When she entered her new apartment, the pictures were on the wall, the dishes were in the cabinet, the furniture was in place. The walls were freshly painted and the windows were open wide, even in winter, because the apartment was so warm.

The family gathered to admire her new home, to comment on the elevators at each end of the building, to marvel at how close she was to shopping, to scold her for not having taken their advice and moved years ago. My mother found the nuts and cookies just where they should be. The paper plates and the napkins were right there. She put up the old kettle for tea. "Does anyone want instant?"

So, if you're looking for Mrs. Siegel, don't go to Seventy-Seventh Street. You won't find her there. Mrs. Siegel is receiving company at home, apartment 4G, on Bay Parkway.

Mrs. Naomi Siegel died August 21, 2002, just one week before her ninety-fourth birthday, and less than a week after having moved into an assisted-living facility in Rockville Center, New York.

The House in the Middle of the Block

MARTA'S HOUSE WAS a well-kept two-story building in the middle of our block, with a sidewalk in front and a long driveway that led to the paved backyard. Marta and her family owned and occupied the whole building. The front of the house had a small square of earth surrounded by a wrought-iron fence, where her sister grew roses. Standing in the middle of the small garden was a plaster statue, about the size of an eight- or nine-year-old child, of a black man wearing white riding breeches, a white shirt, red cap, vest, and bow tie. He extended a lantern in front of him, and his body was bent forward at the waist. He seemed to be peering into the distance for the horse and its rider, who would soon be galloping back from Staten Island or the Bronx. The statue was chipped and gouged in several places and the black face was pocked by white extrusions.

During the war, Marta had converted the patch of ground into a "victory garden" and grew vegetables. People who know New York only from Woody Allen movies are surprised at how lovingly many Brooklynites tend their gardens. Even now, with spring only a promise, my Uncle Meyer is planning where in his small backyard plot to put the tomatoes and peppers and the two varieties of squash, and maybe cantaloupes, again. There was no garden in front of our building, only a bit of sad-looking earth that surely had never been turned over for planting.

Occasionally when I was a teenager, my father and I would walk together to the train station, just a block and a half from our house, and we would stop to admire Marta's garden. Marta would sometimes wave to us from a downstairs window. On other days, if she saw me passing by alone, she might come to her front door, always wearing the same old robe in mid-afternoon, and ask me to run to the grocery store or candy store on some small errand. I was always happy to oblige because when I returned she would give me a tip.

I rarely saw Marta's husband, but I knew he was a cop whose beat was the Brooklyn Navy Yard. He died in a waterfront shootout while I was in high school; it was in the newspaper. It didn't occur to me to walk down the block to offer condolences, and I doubt that my parents offered any. Jews and Italians lived side by side, but separately, on our block. We kids went to the same schools and occasionally played street games together, but our families didn't visit in one another's homes.

Marta had three children. The oldest, Jimmy, disappeared for a year when he was a teenager. The local gossip was that he had been sent to live with relatives, or maybe to a correctional facility, or to a mental institution. When he returned, he dressed elegantly, posturing with a cigarette holder, a pale scarf around his neck, his wavy hair bleached blond and combed back. He walked mincingly, theatrically, and might have been laughable had I not seen him torture cats with his cigarette while he invited children to watch. When he was angry, his voice became a shrill, high-pitched screech. Jimmy had an artistic side, too. On Halloween he would fasten together thin balsa wood baskets that he'd gotten from the fruit market and put a candle in the middle, forming a kind of Chinese lantern. He lit the candle and held the lantern close to his head so that the shadows danced along his face. Then he hung it from a branch. It was beautiful.

Marta's second son, Charlie, was three or four years older than I, but if no one else happened to be around, he would invite me to play. When I finally got my first bicycle, a hand-me-down from a neighbor, he taught me to ride. But I never felt comfortable with him. He had a mean streak that sometimes surfaced. When I had to break up a game of punch ball because my mother was calling me to supper, he put a fist in front of my face and let me know the game wasn't going to end until he had another turn "up." I learned from him that the Jews had killed Christ. One day he caught me playing with a wooden sword.

"What've you got there?" he asked.

"I made a sword."

"Yeah, well that sword is in the shape of a cross, and no Jew is going to play with a cross." He snatched it from me and broke it. Charlie followed his father into the police force, and eventually rose to a high position in the police union.

Marta also had a beautiful daughter, Alice, about nineteen years old. She had long dark hair, dark eyes, silky skin. I was learning about Egypt in school, and in my imagination Alice could have been an Egyptian princess—until she spoke, that is, and pure Brooklynese flowed from her mouth. Marta's sister Agnes also lived in the house. She and Marta looked much alike. They were both short and rather shapeless, with undisciplined hair. There was nothing alluring about either of them. I most often saw Agnes leaning out of an upstairs window, smoking.

Even now, many decades later, I can remember the neighborhood's obsession about what went on in Marta's house, why so many strangers were seen coming and going throughout the day and into the night. There was special interest in the venetian blinds on the first-floor windows. The blinds were sometimes up, sometimes down, in what looked like a random pattern. The men who hung out in front of Izzy's candy store were convinced that the patterns were not random and that the blinds were signals for potential customers: One up, two down: "No room at the inn." Two up, one down: "Y'all come." Three down: "Father is at home—closed for the day." There was even speculation that if you knew the code, you could tell which of the principals was available, depending on the exact configuration of the blinds. None of my informants actually knew the code, but they were nonetheless certain it existed.

When I was well launched into adolescence, I developed a consuming interest in Marta and her establishment. I was too timid to ask my father about it, but during a family gathering I pulled my Uncle Meyer aside and, in a whisper, I broached the topic.

"I can tell you all about Marta's," he said, in a very loud, mischievous voice that made me cringe. "I used to deliver her groceries when

I worked at the A & P. She always gave the delivery boys tips, nice tips." He winked slyly when he said that and looked over at his wife to be sure she had heard him. "Of course, I personally never got past the kitchen," he said. "But the other delivery boys told stories, in-ter-est-ing stories." I didn't know whether to believe my uncle. He liked to tease, and he was obviously putting on a performance for my aunt, who paid no attention to it.

My father married into a family where table pounding, loud arguments, and hyperbole were as necessary to life as pickled herring and boiled potatoes. He couldn't compete in this environment. He was a quiet man whose greatest pleasure was in doing things for others. That is why it is amazing that it was he who finally cleared up the mystery surrounding Marta's house.

As a teenager, I often goaded my father into arguments. I attacked any idea he held reverently, plunging him into discussions about middle-class materialism (though he struggled to keep our family afloat while working two jobs), about respect for one's parents, about bigotry and racism. The topic mattered little. I prodded and probed until my father, in despair, would say, "All right. You win. Pick up the marbles." Then, feeling rather empty and not at all triumphant, I would slink off to regret my victory.

On the day I finally learned the truth about Marta's house, I had been especially obnoxious. I don't recall whether I had gotten a bad grade on a school examination, or was feeling despondent because I couldn't work up the courage to call a girl for a date, but I do recall that on that day I was certain that life was meaningless, school was impossible, girls were unfathomable, my pimples were unconquerable, as was my shyness, and that no one, including my family, truly understood me. I accosted my father in the kitchen and went through my spiel. He listened quietly and then, rather than utter his predictable pronouncement about picking up the marbles, he reached into his pocket and thrust a five-dollar bill at me.

"Here, take this," he said.

"What for?" I asked suspiciously. "I earn my own money."

"This is for something extra, so maybe it will be possible to live in the same house with you. Take the money, and use it."

"What am I supposed to do with the five dollars?" I asked.

My father stuttered when he was agitated. His face was bright red and he was stuttering now. "All right. I'll spell it out. For the past months you've been impossible. You've been cranky and irritable. I think I know why. Take the money, and go visit Marta's establishment."

"Pop, what are you saying? What do you know about Marta's? How do you…? How do you know what goes on there?"

My father fidgeted and didn't look directly at me. "In my bachelor days, when I lived on the East Side," he said, "I used to go there sometimes. We all used to go."

My eyes widened in disbelief. This couldn't be my father. I was incredulous and mute. He got up to leave. Pushing the money toward me, he said, "There's no need to mention any of this to your mother." I remained behind for a moment, too surprised to react, and then I, too, left the room. The five-dollar bill was still on the table.

I never learned the code of the venetian blinds, and I never entered Marta's house. After graduating from college I married and moved out of state, first to attend graduate school and then to begin my teaching career. My father and mother remained in the same Brooklyn apartment. One afternoon in 1966, I was summoned from my classroom. My father had died of a heart attack. He was sixty-three. I flew in for the funeral and was at the apartment helping my mother go through some of his things when we had a surprise visit. Marta had put on a dress and come to our apartment. For a moment I didn't recognize her. I had never seen her fully dressed before. She was holding a bunch of flowers. She stood at the door and offered them to my mother. She wouldn't come in. "I'm sorry for your loss," she said. "I just wanted to tell you what a good man Abe was."

Louis and Me

LOUIS'S VOICE DWARFED even the pearly tones of Mr. Lent, my high school public-speaking teacher of the large and nimble Adam's apple. One sonorous laugh and I was ready to give up Lent for Louis and to follow this new speaker of the word.

Louis had another attraction. He was black. I was young, Jewish, and sure that intolerance and bigotry would vanish now that my generation was leaping into maturity in the early 1950s. We understood the similarities between the black and the Jewish experience. It was no accident that Negro spirituals were grounded in Jewish biblical themes. The signs at country clubs announced that neither Jews nor Negroes were welcome. The Ku Klux Klan held us in common contempt.

I had known only one black person before Louis, a light-skinned woman who for years had been maid and personal nurse to an elderly couple who lived across from us. Gladys doted on the people in her care. When the old man became seriously ill, she moved in with them for weeks. When he died and his wife had to be taken away at last, Gladys tried to rent the apartment for herself. Her own marriage had broken up and she needed a place to live. She knew every crack in the plaster, every neighbor on the block. It was not to be. With the old folks gone, she was no longer *our* Gladys. She had again become one of *them*, and they don't belong.

Louis was the first black to teach at New Utrecht High School. Like Mr. Lent he was a teacher of speech and drama. When he announced tryouts for a production of *Our Town* during my senior year, I eagerly auditioned. We practiced interminably, evenings and weekends, all for two performances. The Saturday before the play opened, after we had rehearsed all morning, I invited Louis to rest in our small apartment just two and a half blocks from the school.

"You're sure it will be all right with your parents?"

"Sure. My father's working and my brother's playing at a friend's house."

The apartment was empty when we got there. Louis lay down on my bed and for a moment I took my brother's. When I was sure he was sleeping, I got up and stood guard in the living room to ward off any intrusion. All the street sounds seemed magnified. I could hear the train pulling noisily into the Seventy-Ninth Street station, the boisterous sounds of boys playing punch ball in the street, and the strains of Yiddish spoken in adjoining apartments and buildings.

My mother returned and looked silently at the still form of the black man sleeping in her apartment. When Louis awoke, he found us huddled in the kitchen. My mother offered him a cup of coffee.

"Thank you," Louis said, "but we still have a few scenes to rehearse and lights and props to worry about."

"You should know how important you've become around here," my mother said. "I'll be glad when this play is over and we can be a normal family again."

"Don't worry," Louis assured her, "just a couple more days. Your son will be a big hit. You'll be proud of him."

Louis laughed and a smile broke across my mother's face. "All right, then, I'll even forgive you for dragging him away from his brother's junior high school graduation tonight. We'll be at the theater tomorrow to see the play." I exulted that my mother and Louis had hit it off.

Our Town did not launch me into an acting career. The stage was deeper in Louis's bones. He quit New Utrecht for a bit part in a Broadway play. He told me this in his home where he had invited me for dinner. I had been inside few private homes and I had never before sat at a table with a black family.

Louis introduced me to his wife, an interpreter at the United Nations, and his son, just a year or two younger than I. After dinner, Louis told me about his plans.

"Why are you leaving New Utrecht?" I asked him.

"It's probably foolish," Louis said, "but this is a chance to be on Broadway. Even though it's not much of a part, I've got to give it a try."

The play was called *Springtime Folly*, and so it was. I saw it the second evening and it closed the next. Louis played a butler. It was simply awful, clichéd and banal. I was embarrassed for Louis. I assumed he would be in mourning, but he was surprisingly cheerful.

"Something wonderful came out of it," he told me. "During rehearsals, one of the other members of the cast brought me to a meeting of the Baha'i faith. You can't believe how exciting it was."

Louis's enthusiasm mounted as he spoke about the transformation he had experienced. He invited me to a meeting of the group. "I want you to experience this," he said.

The meeting was in a crowded apartment in Greenwich Village. The living room had been cleared of furniture and we sat on the floor. The leaders spoke of the shared oppression of all minorities, of the need to work for common goals. When we left I commented to Louis that it had seemed more like a political rally than a religious service.

"Yes," he agreed, "because brotherhood is the core of the religion. That's why it's so exciting and why it's come to fill my life."

"Louis, don't you think that in embracing this new faith you sacrifice something in return—your family's Catholicism, for example?"

"What I lose are things that kept me apart from others. What remains is brotherhood, love."

"It sounds too easy. I've heard this stuff before, and it always costs too much for this kind of brotherhood."

"But you will come to another meeting?" Louis asked, or rather, insisted.

I did go to a second meeting and was struck by its sameness to the first. I told Louis I would not go again. He was disappointed, but his own ardor was not diminished. "Someday you'll be ready," he said.

I didn't see Louis again in New York. I heard that he had separated from his wife and immersed himself increasingly in the faith. I left New York to do graduate work and eventually to teach in the Department of Communication Disorders at the University of Minnesota.

Ten years after that last meeting, I was startled to recognize Louis in the lobby of a Chicago hotel. I was there for the annual speech and hearing convention.

"Louis! How are you? What are you doing here?"

"I've been attending this conference," he told me. "I'm a speech pathologist. I went back to school and got another degree, and I work in Chicago."

"You, a speech pathologist too? That's wonderful."

I waited for Louis to acknowledge my professional accomplishments. I had begun to publish in prestigious journals, had been invited to report on my research at this conference. I was disappointed. He asked after my health and my family, but not for reprints of my articles. I didn't see him again at the conference.

Several years later, one of my students stopped to talk with me after class and somehow I discovered that she was a recent convert to the Baha'i faith. I mentioned Louis's name and she glowed with recognition.

"You know Louis," she exclaimed. "He's a great man. A leader in the faith."

"What is he doing now?" I asked her. "Last time I saw him he was a speech pathologist in the Chicago area."

"He works for the church. The church sends him to integrate areas where there's a need for either a black or a Baha'i presence. He often speaks at college campuses. He'll be here soon. I'm helping to organize his visit."

I arranged to meet him at the Walker Art Center, close to the home of his host family. We sat on a wooden bench in the middle of one of the large exhibition halls. He was noticeably uneasy. We both were. Perhaps it was the wrong setting: the high ceiling, stark white walls, marble floors, large, disquieting modern paintings. Perhaps it was only that we had drifted apart. We fidgeted a moment in each other's company, and then, abruptly, he spoke.

"Jerry, are you happy? Truly happy?"

I didn't know how to answer, but it didn't matter. He pressed on. "I'm asking whether you've found the only true happiness—the peace that comes from a spiritual union with God."

I made some desultory response, but Louis wasn't listening. He had a message to convey.

"I'm so glad to see you again," he said. "I think of you often. There are things I've been wanting to tell you, things that go back to when I first met you at New Utrecht High School. When I started teaching there, I knew that most of the students would be white and Jewish, and that you would look down on me. But I was prepared to be despised. I had an ample supply of anger to ward off your bigotry and condescension."

"That's not the way it was at all, Louis. I was thrilled to be in your play and to have you visit my house. At first I wanted to show how liberal I was, but that vanished as I got to know you. Working with you on *Our Town* was one of the great experiences of my life."

"I know," he said. "That's what messed with my mind. I was confused by the warmth and affection from you and some of the other students. Something was wrong. My foundations were wrong. I hadn't anticipated that people like you and I could become friends. That shook me. Anger didn't prepare me for that. Then, when I found Baha'i, I understood that we didn't need to be suspicious of each other. Blacks, whites, people of all faiths don't have to remain in religious ghettoes protecting their pasts. The future belongs to all of us, in Baha'i, if only we embrace it. That's what I've been wanting to tell you all these years."

He spoke intensely, his voice still rich and resonant. He started softly but couldn't contain himself. I remembered the music of his voice and how enraptured I had been when I first heard his laugh, a laugh that charmed my mother, as well. I remembered, too, the others over the years who had offered me salvation, the men at the gates to Brooklyn College who gave out free copies of the New Testament to those Jews who promised to read it; the born-again student who, out of affection, tried to show me the path to eternal life, the same evangelical path that she had joyously chosen. The airwaves were full of missionaries dedicated to bringing us into the fold:

"Jews, beloved of Christ, why do you turn from him? He is the savior your prophets foretold. Open your hearts and receive…"

Indeed, salvation is at hand. All that is asked, Jews, is that you set aside your four-thousand-year-old passion. So simple, so predictable, and so terribly sad to hear that familiar note in Louis's voice. Louis looked at me inquiringly, and understood my silence.

In 1976 my family and I traveled to Israel for the first time and toured the beautiful Baha'i temple in Haifa. The young woman who instructed us to remove our shoes was an American. When I asked her if she knew of Louis, she responded as if I had uttered an incantation. Of course she knew of him, would love some day to meet him. Did I know him? Had I met him, personally?

Why yes, I did know Louis, a long time ago, in the magic circle of the theater where all things are possible. I knew him in the timid and tentative way of two people from different backgrounds discovering a bond of affection, and rejoicing that such a discovery is possible. I knew him when I was a young, unsettled teenager, crossing into the emotional world of a black adult not so far removed from the same turbulence. For a brief time our lives converged, but then we went different ways and each encounter seemed to drive us further apart. Louis offered love and brotherhood, but the terms of the offer widened the gap rather than drawing us closer.

It has been many years since our trip to the temple in Haifa and I've not seen or heard of Louis since. I've mentioned his name to at least one other Baha'i, but it had lost its magic. She didn't recognize it.

Not long ago I read in the newspaper about a scientific discovery that was being offered as a solution to racial strife. The scientists in a certain laboratory had developed a substance to bleach the color of one's skin so that it would not be possible to distinguish between blacks and whites. The formula was being tested. Such, ultimately, is the solution offered by those who would complete Creation by fashioning us all in the same color, or size, or shape; or by insisting that to love one another we must share the same beliefs. It is seductive in its simplicity. Fortunately, those who offer it have no dominion over the awesome variety with which the world is endowed. Otherwise, there would not be the infinite wonders of nature, nor the likes of Louis and me.

Auspicious Beginning

HOT, HOT, HOT. It was 94 degrees, the hottest day that summer of 1953, and the humidity was not far behind. Alas, the air-conditioning at the Hollywood Manor was broken and in its place were two feeble fans that barely moved the warm air. The groom sweltered in his rented tuxedo (pajamas underneath because the wool trousers scratched) and gray fedora. Gray fedora? With formal attire? Yes, you had to have been there. Earlier, as he had been leaving the apartment where he lived with his parents, he was stopped by Mr. Reiff, landlord, elder, and guardian of religious observances.

"Jerry," he croaked, "where's your hat?"

"Here, in my pocket," the young man replied, pulling out a black skullcap.

"No, no," Mr. Reiff insisted. "Not your yarmulke, your hat."

The groom, on his way to be married, wilting in the heat, was not interested at that moment in exploring the difference between hats and skullcaps, both of which cover the head and therefore signify obeisance to God according to Jewish custom.

"Mr. Reiff, I don't own a hat. I never wear one. I have only the yarmulke which I will put on as soon as I reach the chapel. Better, I'll put it on now, and I have another should this one fall off. Please, Mr. Reiff, they are waiting."

Mr. Reiff, who in winter shoveled the coal into the furnace himself each morning, who changed the washers in the sink without turning off the water main, who repaired locks with wooden matchsticks, who walked two miles to the market to buy a live chicken at two cents off the pound, whose beard looked like an unraveled wool sweater, who guarded the stoop to his building as though it were the entryway to Fort Knox, and who had always felt obliged to fill in the gaps in Jerry's religious education, especially as it pertained to matters of observance—this Mr. Reiff was obdurate. He barred the way.

"You don't go to your wedding without a hat. Under the chuppah you got to wear a hat." It was getting late. Cars for the wedding party were blocking traffic in the street in front of the house. The groom's father retreated into his apartment and reappeared wearing a hat. Mr. Reiff was surprisingly agile. In an instant he too had ducked into his apartment and reappeared with a gray fedora and placed it on Jerry's head, where it can still be seen in all of the wedding pictures, two sizes too large, oddly contrasted with the black coat and tails and ruffled shirt.

Finally, they raced to the waiting cars and were on their way. At the Hollywood Manor, the wedding party had gathered, the young women lovely in their gowns, mothers and grandmothers lovely in the way of mothers and grandmothers. The groom's attendants wore formal white, without fedora, since Mr. Reiff's influence could not extend so far. The bride's European-born father, however, appeared with a suitable hat.

When the guests arrived and the wedding party was assembled under the chuppah, the rabbi/cantor began the service. While he is clearing his throat, it must be acknowledged that this rabbi/cantor was the subject of impassioned discussion between the two families before the wedding, discussions not always conducted in the spirit of two families about to merge through marriage. The bride's family desired a large, *freylikh* (joyous) wedding with all the adornments due their only daughter. This meant chopped liver, soup, salad, chicken, choice of dessert, and a rabbi who was also a cantor. The groom's family, concerned about their finances, were content with a smaller freylikh wedding, without chopped liver, and either a rabbi or a cantor, but not both. These and other such discussions dominated the weeks leading up to the wedding. The bride and groom, who were very young, left these weighty matters to their parents and avoided controversy whenever they could. There were discussions, more discussions, compromises, but the rabbi/cantor was not negotiable. He was a stranger to both families but had been selected by the bride's father, a house painter, on the strong recommendation of Little Jack, also a painter. "This is a cantor," said Little Jack, "whose voice has rich color and whose high notes are sung with unvarnished clarity." Perhaps it was the humidity and the heat but now, at the chapel, his voice came out discordant and strident. He sounded rather like paint that had been improperly strained and stirred, leaving unsightly runs and lumps.

The ceremony was soon over, however. The wine cup was smashed by the groom to the cheers of all assembled—Mazel tov! Mazel tov!—and all adjourned to the dining room and the hot soup. The meal was served first class and the guests ate and drank with a will, despite the heat. The bride's parents beamed as quantities of food disappeared, drowned in bottles of seltzer. Coats and jackets came off. Chicken, potatoes, derma, peas, and ices went in, and the "freylikh" became truly freylikh.

The bride and groom ate the first slice of cake, with the photographer under their noses, and waltzed the first waltz. They were joined by parents and then relatives as Uncle Danny, self-appointed master of ceremonies, enticed everyone onto the floor. Forgotten were the disputes about who would pay for what and who would invite how many of whom. The flowers they had argued about looked fresh and impartial. The groom's father's cigars were adequate. The half empty bottles of liquor were disappearing into purses and pockets. The young people were dancing fox-trots, tangos, and rumbas and finally a hora that coaxed the old ones back onto the floor. Who would have thought that Aunt Mamie could dance like that? The bride's brothers danced too. They held each other stiffly as they executed their one-two-three, one-two-three.

Good will flowed. Becky spoke to Harry for the first time in a decade. Sam acknowledged Eva and a smile passed between them. The groom's father and the bride's father clasped hands and for a moment seemed poised to join the brothers dancing across the floor. Grandmother Annie wept for joy, and for sadness, remembering her husband, Nathan. The bride's mother wept too, as she did on all such occasions, solemn and joyous, recalling her firstborn who had died so suddenly and so young. As the newly married couple flowed around the dance floor, outstretched arms pressed envelopes on the groom containing cash, checks, and savings bonds. "Thank you. Thank you." A gaily tossed head beamed as a face and an envelope swept by, the envelope soon tucked into a bulging pocket.

Finally, the band packed its instruments, the remaining bottles disappeared from the tables, and the guests trundled into the cooling evening shouting good wishes to the young couple. At last the bride and groom were to be alone, off for a honeymoon at Lake George after a night in Manhattan. Artie had the car waiting, bags already in the trunk. Hugs and kisses to the last guests and family.

"The cake, Mom. Don't forget the cake," said Eileen, the new bride. "Take it home and put it in the freezer. And don't forget my wedding dress. I'll get it from you when we get back."

The groom, shorn of fedora, tails, ruffles, and scratchy trousers (and the pajamas), a youth again, fresh in the face, called out, "Bye everybody. Thank you. Thanks for everything." Then, as an after-thought, he thrust the bulging stack of envelopes at his father. "Pop, keep this in a safe place. I don't want to take all that money with me. You can count it if you want to, and see who gave what. No. Better wait until we return and we'll look together."

All right, it's true, he was young, but why did he give the money to his father rather than his father-in-law? Didn't he trust his wife's family? Hadn't they hired the band, paid for extra guests, engaged a cantor/rabbi, arranged for two kinds of dessert, spared nothing, asked for nothing except that the wedding be freylikh? Such thoughtless-ness. But wait, these are our children. Married, but still children. This is no time for recriminations. Let them embark on their honeymoon and their new life. There will be time later to remind them of family obligations and what's proper and right. When they return there will be time to talk. Send them off with a toast.

L'chaim, children. *L'chaim*, everybody.

Across the Ocean to Iowa

THE LONGEST JOURNEY is said to start with a single step, but even a single step can be a long journey. Witness the first, tentative steps of the toddler; the exuberant step that crushes the glass under the wedding canopy. It was a gigantic step that took Eileen and me out of our familiar environs in Brooklyn for the first time, and to Iowa City, Iowa.

"To *vere*?"

"Iowa. In the Midwest."

"I-O-VEY?"

"Yes, Iowa. Where the tall grass grows."

We were both young, just married, and the first of our families to move away from New York. It is easy to forget that Eileen's parents and my grandparents had made the much-more-wrenching departure from Eastern Europe. Once settled in New York, it was as though they had always been there, entrenched firmly in their neighborhoods, venturing no further than an occasional excursion to Prospect Park, the cemetery in Queens, the beach, or Manhattan.

My mother and father were American born. My grandparents rarely talked about the old country. There was no sweet nostalgia for that life. I had to learn later, from novels and histories, about the conditions that drove that earlier generation to abandon homes and relatives and come to America. They spoke with accents of distant lands, but they identified tenaciously with America, and cast no backward glances. Life had begun at Ellis Island.

Many of my friends have been avidly researching family trees that go back hundreds of years. I can trace back one or two generations at most, only imperfectly, and then, after a gap of several thousand years, find my origins recorded in splendid detail in the Hebrew scriptures. I experience an odd sense of disconnectedness, a kind of amnesia that leaves the distant past fully intact and the recent past skimpy and incomplete. My family history consists of tales of pogroms, expulsions, decimation, but these traumas were visited on nameless forebears, not persons I can identify. The faces of my ancestors were archetypes rather than snapshots from family albums. I trace kinship with time and events more than with personages.

Our decision to go to Iowa was greeted as though we were the first to travel to the unknown, and in a sense that was true. Those earlier adventurers at least knew that there would be other Jews in New York and that there would be streets, whether lined with gold or not. But what could be expected in Iowa? Prairies, cornfields, dusty roads, and strangers who thought Jews had horns. Iowa was a thousand miles beyond the last subway stop. Why go there, so far from home? What could possibly be in Iowa that wasn't more abundant in New York?

I had been involved in theater and public speaking in high school. I entered Brooklyn College thinking about a career in radio. That vision was quickly daunted when I took the mandatory "oral pedagogy" examination for entering freshmen and was informed that I had an oratorical disease—I spoke with a Brooklyn accent. I waved my public-speaking medal like a magic amulet in front of the examiners. It had no power over the protectors of the English language who stood guard at these portals of learning. I was required to take a course in remedial speech, there to learn to pronounce *nyew* rather than *noo*; *cante_loop_* rather than *cantalope*; *Lawn Island* rather than *Long Gyland*. It was demeaning, but fateful because the professor who taught this class cared not one whit about dental placement during pronunciation of *t* and was not horrified at *deze* and *doze* for *these* and *those*. He was a student of general semantics and stuttering, and a member of the faculty in speech disorders. He was small, almost tiny, had surprisingly fair skin and bright red hair, and spoke in a quiet, hushed voice that hinted at rare secrets and shared confidences. Oliver Bloodstein (he invited students to call him by his first name, but only the most brazen did) had received his PhD in speech pathology from the University of Iowa, a school with a towering reputation in the field of speech pathology.

The reigning sage at Iowa was Wendell Johnson, a Midwestern farm boy, a severe stutterer most of his life, and now a brilliant protagonist for a theory of stuttering that insisted that the original cause of the problem was not in the speaker, but rather in the attitudes of anxious parents who effectively convinced the child to be hesitant, to speak cautiously, to fear imperfection. Johnson likened the stutterer to the centipede who, having eaten of forbidden fruit, tries to reason logically which leg to extend next, or to the tightrope walker who thinks about keeping his balance and thereby loses it. Johnson had a wonderful way with words: stuttering is what the stutterer does in trying not to stutter again; stuttering starts in the ear of the listener rather than the mouth of the speaker; in stuttering, the patient always has more than two legs.

Soon after registering in Bloodstein's class, I decided to become a speech pathologist. It was a career that seemed to offer all the ingredients I valued. It involved service to handicapped persons. It dealt in human motivation and behavior. As a speech pathologist I could be a scholar, a healer, a student of behavior. The raw materials of speech pathology were people and words, the two things I loved best.

I barely survived my first year at Brooklyn College, earning dismal grades in all my courses except the two semesters of speech with Bloodstein. I became involved in college theater and enjoyed the intimacy and the license for eccentricity that theater people accorded themselves, but always felt on the fringe of this group. In the midst of their flamboyance I was timid. I began taking courses in speech pathology, psychology, sociology, human development, and my abilities as a student expanded. I received some recognition for my writing skills in social sciences. It was that success, finally, which convinced me to specialize in speech pathology. Years later I discovered that Wendell Johnson had characterized himself as a writer who wandered into the field of speech disorders.

I graduated from Brooklyn College, turned twenty-one, and married Eileen all within one week in June. In the fall I entered the MA program in speech pathology at Brooklyn College and took courses in the evening while working as a teletypist in Greenwich Village during the day. I typed papers during my lunch hour on a pay typewriter that H. L. Mencken and Dylan Thomas had used.

Eileen also worked and went to school at night. We saw each other in the morning while making the day's sandwiches, and on weekends while cleaning the apartment and visiting family. I completed my course work in less than a year, took comprehensive examinations, and wrote a master's thesis on stuttering under the guidance of Oliver Bloodstein. Now I was at a juncture. Dr. Goldstein, a longtime family friend and physician, offered to set me up in private practice in one of the rooms in his office. Dr. Rabinowitz, the orthopedist who had operated on my foot when I was six years old and probably saved my life, hinted at a similar arrangement. There were also hospitals and clinics where I might have started out to build a career as a therapist.

A few years earlier these possibilities would have seemed almost too good to hope for, but they were no longer enticing. It dawned on me that I could go further, have a career in teaching and research, publish in books and journals for others to read and study, as I had been doing these past years. There was no PhD program at Brooklyn College or I might have stayed on. I had to look elsewhere. Iowa, across those vast cornfields where Oliver Bloodstein had studied, beckoned. I was accepted into the doctoral program. Our parents were proud, but also stunned. We were leaving. The children were really leaving—only for a while, of course, until I finished my degree; then we would surely return. But still, we were leaving. We were to travel into the interior of America, beyond the skin and outer extremities, into the heartland.

It took two cars to bring us to the airport. Uncle Meyer brought my parents and several other relatives. Eileen and I squeezed in with her mother and father and two brothers, Julius and Norman. My father-in-law lost his way and reached the airport late. Meyer had been there for an hour. We had barely enough time to check in and hurl goodbyes at our parents before we were forced to board, the plane's propellers already turning. Once inside, I rushed to the bathroom, sick from the anxiety that we would surely miss the plane, and the even-greater anxiety that, in our hurry, we had forgotten to say goodbye to someone. There would be no one to meet us when we arrived in Iowa. There would be no familiar faces. The long voyage had begun.

The plane landed in Iowa several hours later—how long a trip was it in those days, in 1954? I looked at the flat landscape, and for a moment mistook the few airport buildings for the city itself. We took a cab to the Davis Hotel, where we spent the next two weeks while we searched for an apartment. Finally, we found a dismal apartment above a garage. The caretaker was anti-Semitic and alcoholic. One of the other tenants got drunk one night and came after us with a shotgun. "You Goddamn Jews!" In town we were accosted by a kindly man who asked, "Are you Jewish? We like our Jews in this town." We heard the expression "Jew him down" for the first time, and heard it spoken by Jews as well as gentiles. We had little money and lived on corned-beef hash (ten cents a can) and learned 120 ways to prepare fatty ground beef from a US Government publication. We attempted pork because it was cheap, but that was too much. I couldn't tolerate it even though I came from a nonobservant home.

For two years Eileen worked odd jobs to augment my fellowship. In our last year, she enrolled in college herself to complete the education she had begun in New York.

At first, the whole tenor of the university was different and alien. At Brooklyn College the classroom was often a battlefield, with students vying with each other and the professor to talk, argue, dispute. In Iowa, decorum ruled. Discussions were uncommon. One of my instructors would ask, "Any questions?" and immediately look down at his notes. Another faced the blackboard throughout his lectures and never made eye contact with the students. The other students all seemed more qualified, better prepared for doctoral study. I hung on. I wrote a few good papers and made a good oral presentation. I learned to modulate my New York humor. My psychosomatic hoarse voice cleared and I began to smile again. I began to think I would succeed.

In my last year I worked on my doctoral thesis and traveled to New York to collect data. I was uneasy now traveling the subways and uncomfortable with the loud, boisterous voices of my family. Why did they have to shout? Why were they always arguing? They all sounded like immigrants, just off the boat. My relatives were uneasy with me, too. They gathered dutifully at my parents' house to see me, but they had to test me, to see whether I'd gone snobbish on them with my advanced degrees. They called me "Doc" and watched to see how I would accept their gibes.

My in-laws were especially insistent on knowing when we would end our gallivanting and return home. Now that I would be a doctor (some kind of doctor), why couldn't I finally set up an office in New York? There were already plenty of teachers and there's no living in teaching. Enough. It was time to come home. I had to explain that we would not be coming home—at least not yet. I was not the kind of doctor who would open a private practice. I wanted to do research, and would have work in a college or university. Most of the programs were in the Midwest. When I finished at Iowa, we would probably go to some other Midwestern city. It strained credulity. Things had gone hard for Eileen's family in the past three years. Eileen's parents became strident. They had been abandoned. A note of blame entered their voices, and of accusation: It's because of us you won't come back. You don't want to be near your family. My parents had some of the same misgivings.

I protested that we had no choice; I had to go where the career dictated, but even as I did I was relieved not to be swept up in the family problems, and happy to have a reason—a need—to move on with our own lives. From Iowa we went to North Dakota, then to Kansas, and finally to Minnesota. It took many years before I could admit to myself, to say nothing of my family, that we would not be returning to New York.

Before we left for Iowa, we had to make a ceremonial visit to Aunt Ida. Ida was the successful sister who had come first to the United States and later sent for my mother-in-law, Rose. Ida had married a wealthy clothing manufacturer who owned a factory in New York's Garment District and lived in some luxury. Rose was forced to work all of her life, leaving her children with a housekeeper when they were very young. She worked in her brother–in-law's factory, another sewing-machine operator scrambling to make a living on piecework. As she became older, she had to plead for her job against the new immigrants looking for work. It was humiliating and bitter.

Still, before leaving for Iowa, it was necessary that we call on Ida. She was already old and her mind did not remain long focused. Her apartment was dark and cool, all of the heavy drapes drawn. The furniture was plush. Ida herself was large and overstuffed. She sat regally in a chair with a high back and we were brought in and introduced.

"Ida, this is your niece, Eileen. Rose's. And her new husband, Jerry. They got married last year. You remember the wedding."

Ida didn't respond.

"They've come to say goodbye. They're going far away. To Iowa."

Ida brightened. She looked surprised. "To *vere*?"

"Iowa. In the Midwest."

Ida stirred herself and leaned forward. She was still puzzled. "I-O-VEY?"

"Yes, Iowa. Where the tall corn grows."

She pondered that silently. Then it seemed to connect with something in her own distant memory.

"Oh. You have to go on a ship to I-o-vey?"

She faded again, and sank back into the plumped-up coolness of the chair and the room. She died soon afterward, while we were in Iowa, a thousand miles away. She had been right, of course. It was an ocean, an enormous ocean of culture and experience that we had to cross on our way to Iowa.

You Shoulda Been There: A Linguistic Guide for Children Whose Parents Grew Up in New York

MODERN SOCIAL SCIENCE has taught us that the most important thing between parents and their children is communication. In former days it was thought that the most important thing was that children should respect their parents, help and honor them, but those attitudes are old-fashioned. Those very children on whose behalf we worked two jobs, and scrimped to pay their tuition—because of whom we didn't go on vacation until we were too old and tired to go on vacation—those same children have become college professors and social scientists. And they have proved in the best scientific journals that the whole time we were raising them, we didn't truly understand how to "communicate."

Proper communication with one's children is a problem for every devoted, anxious, guilt-ridden parent, but it is especially problematic for parents who grew up in New York City and then moved away to Yechupitzville. Every generation creates its own dialect. Parents who struggled to master high school French or Spanish and now have three children spaced by a few years, must become trilingual. The children of these parents have a special challenge—they simply do not understand the dialect of their New York mothers and fathers. That is why this guide has been prepared, to clarify the terms and the vernacular with which their parents grew up. And, for the older generation, it is a test of acculturation. How many of these terms do you still remember? If you are slipping, it may be time for you to visit Uncle Joe and Aunt Esther back in Brooklyn.

PLACE TERMS

North and south do not exist in New York City. There are terms like "Eastern Parkway" or the "West End," but these are proper names, like Fannie or Gertrude, and have nothing to do with direction. New Yorkers use more generic directions. For example, to get to the new library you: Go to Izzy's candy store, turn toward the paint store, and wait for the bus. Then you tell the bus driver where you want to get off, and he'll holler when it's your stop. Of course, Izzy's candy store closed twenty years ago, but it is still his corner. And the paint store is now a delicatessen. Also, the bus drivers frequently don't understand English, and even if they did, what makes you so important that they should announce your stop? They have problems of their own.

Here are some other place terms that may not be familiar to those who did not grow up in New York.

Uptown: Any place you are going to except Coney Island; a place to shop for clothes or go to a "show." You get there by entering the door in the subway station that is marked "Uptown Trains."

Downtown: The other side of the train platform. The side you use when coming home from shopping or the show.

The City: New York, including the five boroughs, but especially Brooklyn, as in the following conversation when my mother first visited us in the Midwest (but it could have been anywhere west of the Hudson).

> Polite stranger: I'm glad to meet you, Mrs. Siegel. Where are you from? *(A stupid question.)*
> Mrs. Siegel: The City.
> Polite stranger: Oh, which city? *(A very stupid question.)*

Candy Store: A corner store that is open seven days a week and sells candy, pretzels (long and twist), sodas, malted milks, frappes, comic books, an assortment of toys and school supplies, cigarettes and cheap stogie cigars, Prince Albert in the can, and newspapers written in English, Yiddish, Italian, and now, Spanish. It is also a social center. Older people hang out in the back room and play pinochle or just talk (what else can older people do?)—mostly about how the country is going to the dogs, and how the kids out front are sending it there. The kids out front harass Izzy, the proprietor, make too much noise, and play hit the penny or box ball. Some of the young people also talk about literature and philosophy. Those are the ones who are really driving the country to the dogs. They will never make it to the back room of the candy store.

Poolroom: A mysterious place. Nobody knows for sure what's in a poolroom because good people don't go into it. Bookies and hoodlums live there and come out at night, when everyone else is sleeping.

House: Where you live. Usually an apartment. Only Hollywood stars and our children live in houses with their own roof and garbage cans.

Stoop: The front steps in front of your building. A place to congregate on warm nights, especially for older people who sit on benches and talk politics. During the day children play games there, like stoop ball, or just sit on the steps and make up fantasies about wonderful things they are going to do and places they will visit when they grow up.

Yechupitzville: Far out! Away from "The City." You can't even get there with three trains and a bus. According to my in-laws, that's where I dragged their daughter, away from family, indoor plumbing, good pumpernickel bread, and civilization.

Our home: A wonderful, quiet, clean, civilized place that used to be in Yechupitzville—until the grandchildren were born there. With the grandchildren there, of course, it is no longer Yechupitzville.

FOODS

Foods are a very important source of communication failure. People who don't live in New York frequently don't know the proper name for many foods. This causes misunderstanding and heartburn.

Roll: The real name for a Kaiser. Who would want to name anything after the Kaiser, anyway?

Bun: The proper name for a roll.

Coffee: A very light-colored liquid made with one part coffee, two parts cream, and sweetener. Only gangsters and bookies drink black coffee. They serve black coffee in the poolroom.

Danish: A special kind of bun, with gooey stuff in it.

Charlotte Russe: Sold in candy stores, it has a cake base topped with a rich mound of swirling white or chocolate whipped cream, pyramiding upward, topped with a cherry. It is eaten slowly by first drawing it close to the mouth so that the whipped cream just barely touches the lower lip and chin, and by then plunging into it until the face is smeared with whipped cream. It is finished by vigorously licking the lips and fingers, and then regretfully consuming the cake.

Egg Cream: A drink made without eggs or cream and purchased in a candy store. Seltzer (with large, energetic bubbles and dispensed from a tap, like barroom beer), thick chocolate syrup, and milk are mixed into a foamy, creamy, sweet drink that cannot be duplicated outside of New York. The air is too thin everywhere else, or perhaps it is too clean.

Custard: Not a famous general, and certainly not an insipid pudding. Custard is the real name for soft ice cream heaped high in a white cone.

Frappe: The cultured name for an ice cream sundae. The final "e" is not pronounced. It's there for decoration, like the cherry on the charlotte russe.

Soda: Syrup and seltzer. No ice cream. If we wanted an ice-cream soda, we'd ask for it. And if we wanted a "phosphate," as they call it in some cities, we'd go to a paint store.

Heartburn: A condition of severe gastric discomfort that occurs when you eat at the other in-laws'.

EXPRESSIONS AND IDIOMS

A Lovely Affair: A wedding or a bar or bat mitzvah that costs a bundle and is distinguished by poor taste and ostentation.

Make the Light: An instruction to turn on the stove or flip a light switch. Nothing is actually made.

Put it up: When a New Yorker says, "Put it up," he means what he says: Up, on a shelf, up there. Not "put it away."

A Wonderful Catch: This is not baseball jargon. It means he's not too bad, but she would have done better with my Lenny.

A Clever Person: Smart, but tricky. Not to be trusted.

APPLIANCES AND MACHINES.

Singer: Grandma or Grandpa's sewing machine, not an entertainer.

Ice Box: A refrigerator, also a "fridge." Not Minnesota, North Dakota, or Upstate New York.

Machine: An automobile.

Dishwasher: Grandma.

Food Processor: Also Grandma, with her wooden chopping bowl and a metal hand-held chopper.

Chutzpah: What it takes to use a term like *"chutzpah"* by people who don't really understand it, and can't pronounce it.

Finally, you children who didn't grow up in New York, when your parents say, "You don't know how good you've got it," what they really mean is: When we were young we had little, because our parents had little to give. We promised ourselves that our children would not struggle and sacrifice and go without, as we had. We promised ourselves you would have a better life. We succeeded and now we are worried. In giving you tennis lessons, music lessons, designer jeans, private schools, and a room of your own in a real house, did we succeed too well? Did we leave you a stoop? Did we crowd your lives with so much we didn't leave room for wonderful fantasies and dreams of your own?

With luck and effort, you children of New York parents, you'll find your own stoop, and the equivalent of our egg cream and charlotte russe. And, who knows, you too may have to learn a new vocabulary as your own children travel to a new generation, to new places, perhaps even to the streets and sidewalks of New York.

North Side Memories

I DON'T HAVE the same bragging rights as the original North Siders, the ones who as youngsters dared each other to sneak into the Homewood movie theater and nearly got caught, who can name every store that used to line Plymouth Avenue, every Jewish family who lived between Knox and Washburn, who knew Rabbi Feller and Ron Meshbesher when they were ordinary children.

My family didn't get to the North Side until 1961 when it was already in transition, but it was still a unique community. We only stayed for two years. When we left, the North Side was in its last gasp as a center of Jewish life in Minneapolis.

I interviewed at the University of Minnesota in the spring of 1961. The position involved a split appointment in two departments that didn't get along with each other. The academic program wasn't distinguished. There was very little ongoing research, and the graduate program was miniscule. Despite these first impressions, in the weeks that followed the weaknesses began to seem like opportunities. The graduate program was undeveloped, but the university was large and prestigious. The departments were so eager for increased research that I could work in any area of the field I chose, and I could expect support for my efforts. And there would be a Jewish community and Jewish education for our children.

What finally turned my mind may have been my first house-hunting tour in the Twin Cities. I was driving along a very unappealing street filled with car dealerships and garages when I passed Abram's Deli on the corner of Lake and Emerson in South Minneapolis. At first I thought it was a mirage. I stopped for a moment and there, right at the meat counter, were slabs of pastrami and corned beef, large kosher pickles, several brands of salami, real rye bread, hal-vah. Then, as I continued along Lake Street, Lake Calhoun loomed up beautiful and tranquil. After having spent years in arid Iowa, North Dakota, and Kansas, the sight of that beautiful lake clinched it for me.

The secretary in my new department, the wife of a divinity student, helped me decide where we would live. When she heard I was looking at apartments on the North Side, she cautioned me, "You wouldn't want to live there. Too many blacks and Jews." That made the North Side irresistible. We found a second-floor apartment on 1426 Penn Avenue. Our immediate neighborhood was mixed. Our landlords, white Presbyterians, lived below us. Jim was apprenticing as a plumber. On weekends he worked as a bartender at Howie's on Broadway. Over a beer, Jim confided that his wife's father was Jewish, and one of the organizers of the Minnesota Communist Party.

Just to the south of us, the McCoys, a black family, owned a single-family house. They were friendly neighbors. They entrusted their children to us when we went to our first Aquatennial parade. Mrs. McCoy sent us off with a gigantic bag of popcorn. That same summer her married daughter came home for a visit. I remarked to Mrs. McCoy how attractive her daughter was. "Yes," she said. "She does look fine. And this trip her color is so good." It hadn't occurred to me that blacks also had variations in color depending on their general health or well-being.

One house north of us lived an elderly couple with deep roots in the Jewish community. They were very hospitable to us and our children and we became quite friendly. When they moved, Mr. Barr sold me his old rolltop desk. I still use it in my study and visitors invariably admire it.

Along Plymouth Avenue there were delicatessens in rich profusion, and Jewish bakeries, and kosher meat markets. For an exciting moment there was the prospect that the Homewood, a theater that had once hosted live Yiddish performances, would reopen. A concert was scheduled featuring pianist Peter Nero but the Minneapolis newspaper went on strike before the program could be promoted and the concert was canceled. The building remained dark.

We were surrounded by synagogues. Beth El was so close we could roll out of bed and be at the front entrance, but we joined Tifereth B'nai Jacob congregation, some distance away. I'm not sure why. Maybe it was like the joke about the Jew who was marooned on a desolate island. When he was found many years later, he had built two synagogues. "Why two?" he was asked. "Oh, that one, the one close by, that's the one I don't go to," he answered.

My friend Jerry Pauker lived in the neighborhood and also taught at the university; we often drove to work together. I was surprised when he told me he had joined one of the Orthodox synagogues. "As long as I'm not going," he explained, "I'd rather not go to an Orthodox synagogue."

Desnick's Pharmacy was on our corner at Penn and Plymouth. In 1985, while I was on sabbatical, I met Bernie Gordon in synagogue in Santa Barbara, California. Bernie had grown up in Minneapolis and had originally owned the store that eventually became Desnick's Pharmacy. Bernie's father was one of the early rabbis at Adath Jeshurun Synagogue in Minneapolis. In Santa Barbara, without a hint of snow, we reminisced about frigid winters and the old North Side community.

Malcoff's and Brochin's competed for our pastrami budget. When I worked late, as I often did those first years in Minneapolis, I would stop off and buy Eileen a pastrami sandwich as a peace offering. Pastrami and sour pickles probably saved my marriage. People's and North Side bakeries still flourished. Sunday mornings, stores were open all along the avenue. Store clerks sat outside on nice days, in front of their shops. We wheeled David and Karen past a stream of admirers who chucked them under the chin, remarked on their good looks, and pressed a treat into their willing hands. Mr. Gold always had something special for our children, and a three-for-a-dollar bargain often turned into four-for-a-dollar when we stepped into Gold's Variety.

In the early 1960s, the North Side was much like the Brooklyn neighborhood I had known as a child. It boasted at least one of every kind of shop: bakery, meat market, fresh fish, cleaning store, shoemaker, delicatessen, greengrocer. There were stories hinted at along Plymouth Avenue. I brought my leather belt to a shoemaker for repairs. When I picked it up a few days later, I was distraught at the poor craftsmanship. The work was sloppy. The stitches were uneven. I was about to complain when I noticed the numbers tattooed on the shoemaker's arm. I took the belt, paid, and left the shop quietly.

We moved from Penn Avenue in 1963. Our landlady had been complaining that our children made too much noise racing across the uncarpeted floors. We tried to quiet them, but it was impossible. The neighborhood had become more tense, too. We heard of drugs openly peddled just a few blocks away. There was a killing. Fewer Jews remained and stores on Plymouth Avenue were moving or closing. David and Karen would start school soon. We had been married for ten years. It was time for this Brooklyn boy to buy a shovel and a rake. In November, we bought a house on Gladstone Avenue in South Minneapolis and lived there forty-two years until, in 2005, we moved to a condominium in Edina.

Our North Side landlords moved not long after we did. They tried, unsuccessfully, to sell the duplex but instead were forced to rent both apartments. One day I read about a Vikings football player who had been cut by the team and was renting a room from a couple in our old apartment on Penn Avenue. The husband came home and found his wife in a compromising situation with the tenant. There was a scuffle and the football player athletically leaped out of the second-story window into the backyard where our children had played, and broke his leg. The report appeared in the main section of the Minneapolis Tribune. I felt brushed by fame.

We were gone from Minneapolis during the 1967–68 academic year. During the summer, the rage that had been unleashed in black neighborhoods in other parts of the country erupted on the Minneapolis North Side. People were beaten. Stores were destroyed. Soon after, the synagogues all closed, merged, or moved to the suburbs. Beth El synagogue became Pilot City, a community center. Others became churches. The old North Side was gone. So, too, was the newer North Side we had known.

Although I and my family were not part of the original, vibrant community I hear about whenever North Siders reminisce, I too mourn its passing. Even in our time, it was a warm and protective place where we were surrounded by signs of Jewish life when shopping, socializing, celebrating the holidays, and simply walking the streets past Jewish stores and institutions. It was an education just to look in the shop windows and to read the postings of upcoming events. It is unlikely we will ever again have a community quite like it in our city. I feel lucky to have been there. Better latecomer than never.

Unanswered Letters

HERBERT GREEN WON a teaching award at Michigan Tech University. I saw the announcement in the Brooklyn College alumni magazine. Herbert and I had been close friends in New Utrecht High School in the late 1940s, when his name was still Greenberg. After graduation we both went to Brooklyn College. He majored in languages and I took French to satisfy the liberal arts requirement. I wasn't especially good in the language, but I was a theater student and had a flair that masked my deficiencies. We took a few classes together but he soon left me far behind.

After college we drifted apart and lost touch. I hadn't communicated with Herbert for more than forty years but after seeing his name in the alumni magazine I dug out my college yearbook and spent some pleasant hours looking through the *Brooklundian* at black-and-white pictures of former classmates, including Herbert, pausing for a moment, just a moment, at my own picture: Thin. Unwrinkled. Dark, wavy hair.

I knew that rediscovering an old friend would not restore my dark, wavy hair, but nonetheless I wrote to Herbert in care of his department. I congratulated him on his award and mentioned that my daughter had done her graduate work at the University of Michigan in Ann Arbor, and I wished I had known he was close by. Herbert sent back a warm letter. He included clippings describing the accomplishments that had led to his award. I learned that Herbert had carved out a special niche for his scholarship that combined French and opera. He remembered my wife, Eileen, and her brother Julius, who had hoped to become an opera singer. I didn't recall that he and Julius had ever met.

Herbert had married in Europe and had one child, a son, but no grandchildren and, he said, no prospects for grandchildren. His wife was not Jewish. There had been some difficult times. Illnesses, emotional turmoil. He revealed all of this in his letter. Herbert seemed genuinely pleased to hear from me and I anticipated a renewed relationship. I responded and included some stories and essays that I'd published.

Many months have passed, and there has been no further word from Herbert. I've reread my last letter to him several times. There are no split infinitives, no hanging participles, nothing I can discover that should have given offense, but he hasn't answered. I've thought about writing to Herbert again, but that seems intrusive, or requires more courage than I can muster. Perhaps it's enough to have been in momentary contact, briefly to have revived a part of the past without creating any emotional attachments or encumbrances, but there remains something incomplete about that last unanswered letter.

I didn't get to ask Herbert Green whether he had ever been to a New Utrecht High School class reunion. The fiftieth anniversary of our graduation has come and gone but no one contacted me about a celebration or reunion. As a matter of fact, I've not had any communication since I graduated in 1949, so I sent a letter to: Dear Principal, New Utrecht High School, Brooklyn, NY 11214, mentioning my whereabouts and asking whether they had been trying to contact me. Lots of celebrities went to New Utrecht: Abe Burrows, Buddy Hackett, the opera singer Robert Merrill, David Geffen. Barney Hyman, the New Utrecht track coach, played the musical saw in the Catskills during the summers. Uncle Meyer was on Barney Hyman's track team.

New Utrecht was large. We had eight hundred in our graduating class and I don't suppose I'd have known many if I had gone to a reunion. Still, I would have liked to have gotten an invitation. I'm not expecting a distinguished alumnus award, but I did win the 1949 public-speaking medal, and represented the school in the American Legion oratorical contest with a speech about Alexander Hamilton, and I have had some professional distinction which might bring credit to my former high school. "Dear Principal" hasn't answered my letter.

More recently, I wrote to Milton Kudlacek. When we were students at the University of Iowa, Eileen and I had an apartment in the same building as Milton, over a garage, across the street from Mr. Braverman's grocery store. Mr. Braverman was our landlord. Milton was majoring in studio arts. He shared his apartment with another student, Tom. To earn extra money he and Tom cooked hamburgers in their kitchen and peddled them illegally to fraternities and sororities on the weekends. We were all quite poor and struggling to survive. A fellow student had a raging argument with his wife while she was in the kitchen making sandwiches. In anger, he flung a tube of liverwurst against the kitchen wall and stalked out. When he returned a little while later, he saw his wife scraping the liverwurst off the wall onto bread for the next day's lunch.

Before Eileen and I graduated and left Iowa City in the summer of 1957, I completed a delicate transaction with Milton. He had produced a set of five watercolors as part of the MFA requirements in the art department—outdoor scenes of a small town in Iowa. We offered to buy the paintings to remind us of our years in Iowa. We had barely any money and could offer Milton only twenty-five dollars. Although he needed the cash, to sell his paintings for five dollars each was too hard on his pride. Instead, we agreed to buy one painting for twenty-five dollars, and he gave us the remaining four as a gift.

Kudlacek's paintings traveled with us from Iowa to North Dakota and then to Kansas, where we gave one of the set as a gift to our friends the Nelsons. In 1961 we moved to Minnesota and the paintings languished in a basement storage closet until, recently, we had the mats and frames changed and hung them once more in the living room. The woman who helped us at the frame shop was quite enthusiastic. She doesn't often get to work with original paintings.

I hadn't thought about Kudlacek for a long time. We had seen him once after we left Iowa. We were traveling from Minnesota to Colorado and stopped at his mother's home in Sioux Falls, South Dakota. Milt had graduated and had moved back home. That was many years ago. Now I wondered whether he had continued to paint. I fantasized that Kudlacek had achieved recognition as an artist and that, like those exciting discoveries on the *Antiques Roadshow* that Eileen watches so faithfully, his paintings—our paintings—might have become valuable.

I searched the Internet and found a Milton Kudlacek in Sioux Falls. It had to be him. I wrote and told him a little about ourselves, and that his paintings were displayed in our Minneapolis home. I thought he'd be delighted to hear from me, and especially to hear about his watercolors. In a reverse of Dorian Gray, he and I would have aged, but not his paintings. I half expected a reply in the return mail but my letter is still unanswered. My letter wasn't returned, so someone must have received and presumably read it. If not Milton himself, wouldn't that person be interested in Milton's paintings?

I also wrote to Roberta Nelson, the owner of the orphaned Kudlacek painting that we left behind in Lawrence, Kansas. Jim Nelson and I had been classmates at the University of Iowa. The Nelsons were gracious and kind and a great comfort those first years when we were newly married and separated from home and family for the first time. We met up with the Nelsons again after we graduated. Jim had taken a teaching position at the University of Kansas, and in 1959 I had a research appointment at the Parsons State Hospital, about 140 miles south of Lawrence. I traveled to the university almost weekly. Eileen and I had our first two children, David and Karen, during that period, and the Nelsons helped us through the unfamiliar trials of parenthood. In 1967, I had a sabbatical at the University of Kansas, in Lawrence. The Nelsons were still there. Our son David joined the Cub Scouts and Jim helped him carve a winning entry for the annual pinewood derby. We left at the end of the academic year, and a short time later Jim died. Eventually we lost touch with Roberta.

David is now married and has children of his own. At about the same time that we rediscovered Kudlacek's paintings, our grandson Jacob proudly showed me the car he and David had carved for the Eagan, Minnesota, pinewood derby. All these memories came together. Now I had to learn what had happened to Roberta. Using the Internet again, I found that she was still in Lawrence, though at a different address. I wrote to her, but that letter too has gone into the void, unanswered and not returned.

I have written other letters that have not gotten a response. It's puzzling. People my age generally have the inclination to remember earlier days, to be curious about folks we knew, and to find pleasure in recalling long-ago experiences. Not all were happy or triumphant, but time has often removed the sting and we can see them in a different light. We can exaggerate and revel in hard times from this distance. More than that, it's affirming to make a connection with our past.

I have developed a theory about why my letters have gone unanswered. It has occurred to me that Herbert and Dear Principal and Milton and Tom are all conspirators in a nefarious scheme. This came to me as I was watching a news program about a local group who broke into the laboratories of the University of Minnesota Medical School and "liberated" animals that were being used in studies of cancer, heart disease, and addiction.

I have concluded that Herbert Green is only posing as a student of the arts when, in reality, he is a leader of an Animal Rights Terrorist Society (ARTS) based in Paris and dedicated to liberating animals from zoos. That's the real reason he learned French. Milton Kudlacek is a sympathizer. His role is to produce shocking paintings of zoo animals being terrorized. His roommate Tom was testing a poisonous chemical additive in Iowa City that was to be given to zookeepers just before the animals were simultaneously set free all over the world. The additive, mixed with hamburgers, is the real reason so many Iowa fraternity and sorority students had a mysterious illness in 1954 that was incorrectly attributed to a strain of influenza.

The FBI became suspicious and Milton destroyed the additive, but he painted the secret formula into the designs on his Iowa paintings. He gave the pictures to me because he had word of an imminent FBI raid. The plan was to retrieve the paintings at a later time, but Milton had a falling-out with his mother after we visited him in Sioux Falls. They were leaning out of an upstairs window, and both fell out. Milton struck his head and could not remember who had the paintings. The terrorists went underground. They learned that I had the paintings when they intercepted my recent letter to Kudlacek.

Roberta Nelson was an innocent victim. The terrorists needed the missing painting in Kansas. They have kidnapped her and are holding her hostage in the basement of New Utrecht High School. Although Dear Principal hates animals, he is also a terrorist (as students have been insisting for some time, but of course no one takes teenagers seriously). He studied education at the University of Iowa at the same time my wife and I were there. He fell in love with Eileen and tried to convince her to run away with him. When she refused, he swore vengeance and joined up with the animal terrorists.

It all fits together. This may be my last communication before I am kidnapped. The terrorists surely won't allow me to receive mail, so any of you who owe me a letter, don't bother trying to write.

On the other hand, my theory may be wrong. Theories often are. Herbert and the others may not be involved in a terrorist conspiracy. They may not even know each other. They may have lost my return address and can't find us. Even though we lived in the same house for forty-two years, we have moved recently. Or, they may have our address and may still fully intend to write when the kids, and then the grandkids, are gone, and they get a free moment. If that is the case, I hope that they remember that postage has gone up again this year. It would be grand to hear from them.

It would be grand to hear from almost anyone other than catalog, credit card, and real estate companies, and petitioners for the multitudes of worthy causes, and political parties, and bill collectors, and distributors of surveys-that-will-only-take-a-few-minutes-of-your-time. It would be grand to hear from all of you. Let us all do what we can to wipe out the glut of unanswered letters. Even those of you who might be involved in the animal-rights movement, send a letter, a real letter, not a polemic or a pamphlet. I promise to answer.

Herbert, and Dear Principal, and Milton, and Roberta, and you others—we had a voice in each other's lives at one time, sometimes a loud and raucous voice. Why not now at least a whisper?

Synagogue Stories

Mr. Mogol

THE TRUTH OF THE MATTER IS I really don't know Mr. Mogol well. I never did, but he became very important to me. I suppose it was his voice. His voice was a growl—deep, penetrating, a dark rumble that stood out from the chants and songs in the sanctuary. His voice was one thing, his timing was another. He was always a word or a syllable ahead or behind. When the congregation was singing "*Shema…*" he was already on "*Yisrael…*" With that voice and that timing, his was an inescapable presence. Sometimes I felt I was within the cavern of that deep, hollow rumble that was Mr. Mogol's voice.

As a youngster I studied at a neighborhood cheder near my home in Brooklyn until I reached the age of thirteen and had my bar mitzvah. I remember little of those years except that the small synagogue school was always dark and musty. My family went to services on the High Holy Days but seldom more often than that. I knew I was Jewish. It was announced in the Jewish newspapers at the corner candy stores and in most of the homes I visited; it was announced in the "Kosher" signs in the butcher shops; it was announced by the 85 percent Jewish student body at P.S. 186, my elementary school. There was no question of a Jewish identity.

In Minneapolis it is different. Here a Jew has to seek out an identity, the companionship of another Jew, the signs of his heritage. This is a Christmas-tree culture with Easter bunnies peeking out among the trees. You want your children to know about Jewish life and values; you can't wait for a neighbor to provide a lesson. No. You have to seek it out. So here in Minneapolis I go to the synagogue on the Sabbath. Once I'm there, it feels good. It also feels lonely.

It feels lonely for a couple of reasons. I'm still a stranger here. That's the way it is in a large congregation where more than 1,200 families belong, some second- and third-generation members, but none my neighbors. I enter the sanctuary. I take my seat. I sing my prayers as vigorously as the next person. I listen attentively to the sermon. And when the service is over, I dutifully, even hopefully, wish a fellow congregant a "Shabbat Shalom," and that's it. There are no warm greetings, no one to tell me how glad he is to see me, no old family friend to inquire after my wife and children. I am a stranger among people whose faces and ways are so familiar I feel I must know them, but their friendship eludes me.

Except for Mr. Mogol. That is his special gift. Mr. Mogol is no youngster. When I first became aware of him, he was already into his late seventies. He was retired and his wife had recently died. The synagogue was the mainstay of his existence. On Shabbos he was there without fail. On weekdays, he attended morning and afternoon prayers. Usually some member of the community would pick him up and drive him to shul. Eventually, whenever I was in synagogue, I looked for Mr. Mogol. He became the link between my new home and the old, pious men I had known as a child in Brooklyn. When I came to synagogue, I would locate his rumble and that made me feel welcome. I was in the right place. I searched him out at the end of the Shabbos service to grasp his hand and wish him Sabbath peace. Because of his age and his long acquaintance there, he was something of a celebrity, and I never spoke with him. I was shy, even chagrined that I had endowed him, without his consent or knowledge, with so significant a place in my own imaginings. Occasionally I would be back in synagogue after an absence of several weeks and he wouldn't be there. I felt uneasy. Something was missing. I knew he was old and I became concerned. I had come to count on the unchanging quality of his voice, his ponderous gait, his invariable black suit and tie. We knew nothing of each other, were separated by decades in age, but if Mr. Mogol was there, growl in place, words out of time, I felt as though I had a friend.

Eventually Mr. Mogol truly disappeared. Week after week he was absent from his usual place in synagogue. I asked one of the older members about him. I feared the worst.

"Mr. Mogol? Oh, he's in the Sholom Home. Since his wife died, he don't take such good care of himself, so they took him to Sholom Home. Sometimes he shows up for services, though."

Months passed before I saw him again. It was Yom Kippur and I had almost forgotten him. By now I knew a few people, recognized a few faces that smiled back at me. I felt less alone in synagogue. So I wasn't prepared, there in the hush of the holiest of Jewish days, to hear once again the distant rumble of his prayers tumbling about the synagogue walls. A sense of well-being swept over me. Mr. Mogol was davening, and all was well. This he did for me without even acknowledging my presence on that holy day.

I see Mr. Mogol rarely now. Even occasional trips from the home are daunting. The effort and the excitement…Once in a great while one of his children or grandchildren will bring him to synagogue and there he is watched over like a precious, fragile gift.

But we did finally meet. It was in the Sholom Home. Once a year I volunteer there to sing Jewish songs to an appreciative audience of mostly elderly Jewish residents. I do it with pleasure. The occasion is exciting, with much hubbub, and looking for chairs, and finding a proper stool for me to sit on, and getting the audience settled and facing the right way. This last time, this very year, there was Mr. Mogol himself, dressed in his black suit, black vest, and tie. Short, stout, moving slowly. His face red with effort, his voice gruff with greetings to the other residents. He has come to the concert to hear the professor who plays Yiddish songs. I see him and my face beams. He smiles back, but a little confused. He doesn't know me. No matter. I sing a few songs, glancing always at him. He is enraptured by the music and rises to his feet.

"How about a song from one of the old-timers?" says the social worker who is the master of ceremonies. He looks at Mr. Mogol who is approaching the front of the room. There is applause and an occasional, "What? What did he say?"

Mr. Mogol moves to the microphone. His face reddens. He leans slightly forward and his eyes widen as he portrays the disappointed lover in the Yiddish song he sings. His gravelly voice flows out of him in merriment to all corners of the room. His singing is punctuated by shades of interpretation, by winks and melodic twists as he caresses this song he has known for sixty, seventy years, has sung and heard sung hundreds of times. His face flushed, his body swaying, his voice cracked, he finishes. There is applause. I rush over to him.

"That was wonderful, Mr. Mogol, just wonderful," I tell him, and giving in to an urge I have so long felt, I kiss him on the cheek.

"Oy," he exclaims, surprised, but pleased. "You liked it?" he asks.

"It was wonderful, Mr. Mogol."

He sighs. "I'm glad you liked it." One of the attendants helps him to his chair. He sits, his face red with effort, his eyes half closed, brow glistening with sweat.

"Oy," he says, touching the place where I kissed him. "I'm glad you liked it."

A Cantor for All Seasons

MAYBE YOU THINK the cantor in your synagogue is somebody special. I know how it is. Because it is your cantor, in your synagogue, he can't be ordinary or just plain good. He has to be a musical genius who makes the heavens quake when he so much as opens his mouth. With so many extraordinary cantors coaxing *Moshiach* (the Messiah) from his hiding place, it's a miracle he didn't arrive long ago.

Don't get me wrong. Just because people are vain doesn't mean there is no such thing as a truly exceptional cantor. It just so happens that I know such a one, and it also just so happens that until recently he was the cantor of my synagogue. I can see already that you are smirking and, like the others, you are about to insist on the merits of your own cantor. But hold your horses. Before you jump in, let me tell you about Cantor Amsel. He has a voice, a quality that can't be described. It has to be experienced. I'll prove it to you.

Several years ago we had a cantorial program in my city and the cantors from three synagogues participated. It could have been called the War of the Cantors or the Cantorial World Series. Naturally the congregants from the three synagogues all came to cheer for their own cantor, convinced that he was the best of the lot. Before the program even began there were heated disputes about the relative merits of the performers. From the sound of things, the audience would have been content to spend the evening arguing, without any concert at all.

The concert was held in the sanctuary of my synagogue, Adath Jeshurun, and by the time my wife and I arrived, the room was practically full. People were pushing and shoving to find seats. I saw a bench near the front and off to the side, which was vacant except for a large woman who seemed determined to occupy the entire bench herself.

"Excuse me, lady, are those seats next to you taken?"

She rolled her eyes at such a question, and gestured to the purse, sweater, and fur piece she had strewn across the bench.

"I'm saving for my husband."

"Lady," I said, "how many seats does your husband need? You've got a whole row blocked off."

"Well, I'm also saving for my friends, in case they decide to come."

"Please, lady, the concert is going to start and we have no seats. How about if you let us be your friends and have two seats. You can still save one for your husband."

Grudgingly she collected her belongings into a pile and inclined her body sideways, a signal meaning we were to enter. We pushed, squeezed, and squirmed past her.

The program began with the usual announcements and thank-yous and statements of how the evening wouldn't have been possible without the help of this one and that one—a very long list of names. The audience was becoming restless. Finally, the first cantor.

This one I had heard once before. He sang from his shoes, with low, murky tones. When he trilled a note, it was like he was wiggling his toes. I glanced at my neighbor and she was beaming. Obviously, this was her cantor. He coughed, she glowed. He cleared his throat, she nodded rapturously. She turned to me. "You heard that 'harrumph?' That's from a cantor with a golden throat."

When he was finished with the preliminaries and finally began to sing, do you know what came out of that golden throat? Not a proper cantorial. Not a Yiddish or a Hebrew folk song. No. An operatic aria! In Italian, no less. I couldn't believe it. I leaned over to make a remark to my neighbor, but she immediately shushed me.

"Shh. Can't you hear? The cantor is davening."

What can I say? If that is davening, my grandparents weren't Jewish.

The next cantor had a nice voice, I have to admit, but who could hear him? His voice was drowned out by his face. Every note required a different facial contortion. The eyes, the mouth, the nose—all busily twitching and grimacing.

"If it hurts him so much," I whispered to my wife, "he should give up singing." Eileen refused even to smile but my neighbor on the bench guffawed loudly.

Finally, the moment I had been awaiting. Our Cantor Amsel strode to his familiar pulpit in front of the congregation. The audience sensed something special was about to occur. A hush fell over the crowd. I was about to hurl a hush at my new friend and neighbor, but she had fallen asleep.

"Lady," I whispered, "THE CANTOR is about to begin."

She didn't stir. She lolled there, her body folded like an accordion, her head precariously balanced against the high arm of the bench. I lightly touched her. Still no sign of life. I was about to administer a more forceful jab, or artificial respiration, when she suddenly sat bolt upright. Someone in the audience had coughed and she mistook it for her own cantor singing again.

At last, the moment. Cantor Amsel rocked back on his heels, leaned forward, closed his eyes. Magic ensued. Beautiful, clear, plaintive tones issued, recalling the joy and awe of the Sabbath and the Holy Days. Not only the notes, but the intervals between the notes were melodic and beautiful. This cantor doesn't drown a song. The voice and the prayer blend so that the words sing the melody, and the melody thrusts the words ahead, filled with supplication. It is not proper davening when you hear the cantor but not the prayer. The singer's voice must be as a brush that paints the words, now with delicate and now with forceful strokes, always highlighting the prayer. The words and the music do not compete. They are one.

Our cantor understands this. That is what made him so outstanding that evening. Ask anyone who was there, even my neighbor with the husband and friends who never showed up. Even she was moved to utter a grudging, "Not bad."

But wait, there's more. In her face, and all of the faces in the audience something was happening. Lips were moving. Bodies were swaying. Voices were raised. That, finally, is the essential quality of Cantor Amsel. When he sings, there are a hundred cantors, not one. Whoever is in the congregation becomes a cantor. A nod of his head, a glance in our direction, a change in the rhythm, and we are all transformed into cantors of the first order. Old and young, high-pitched and gravel voiced—all become certain of our ability to reach the most soaring notes, to sustain the most delicate trill, to blend falsetto and full voice. Through Cantor Amsel, you and I and my friend at the concert, we all experience the lilting joy of a cantorial triumph. That, more than the beautiful voice and stirring interpretations, is his greatest gift.

But perhaps you've already heard. Our cantor is leaving us, retiring after thirty years on the same pulpit. The High Holy Days are coming, and he won't be in his familiar place in front of the congregation. How will it feel? Like the first time there are faces missing from the Passover seder. Like an important ingredient missing from a favorite recipe. Like celebrating an anniversary by oneself. I will miss being one of his High Holy Days cantors. When he sang, there was no note I could not reach, no melody too complex. Now that he is going, I am concerned. Not about Cantor Amsel, or even about our congregation. He will be warm and sought after in Florida, and our congregation will find a replacement cantor. But what about me? When I sing in the congregation, when the holidays come and I join in on my favorite melodies, will I ever be so magnificent again?

Mr. Mayberg Reads Torah

MR. MAYBERG READ Torah today, and the Heavens grumbled. Surrounded by young men in their teens, many still his pupils, Mr. Mayberg, wrapped in a huge prayer shawl, inclined his frail and ancient body toward the Torah and, in a quavering voice, read flawlessly. Still, the Heavens protested. It was the Sabbath and Mr. Mayberg, oblivious of all else, consumed entirely by the scrolls in front of him, read Torah. A simple reading: no frills, no melodic twists, no dramatic pauses. Each word uttered lovingly, an echo of the thousands of times he had uttered these same words in the past. The chant hung for a moment over the congregation before rising to become one with the Word.

When Mr. Mayberg reads Torah, the words do not rush out helter-skelter. The angels do not snap up the words to meld and blend them with God's timeless chorus. No, the words are allowed to linger, to float slowly upward. When the cantor davens in his rich and resonant tones, the sounds leap out and reach Heaven the instant they are uttered, or before. Not so with Mr. Mayberg. But why? Could it be that his raspy, trembling voice does not find favor among the heavenly choir? That his unmelodic chants are given slower passage and reluctant entrance because they sound harsh to those celestial ears?

Choir Leader: "Lord, I am having trouble with the heavenly choir. They complain that when Mr. Mayberg sings, they lose the melody, forget their parts. He throws them off."

Lord: "Who is this Mr. Mayberg?"

Choir Leader: "He is a pious man, well into his eighties, who keeps the commandments. For more than forty years he was a teacher in a

Talmud Torah. Now he is retired but still he teaches, the young and the old, whoever would study with him. The young, especially, come to study with him because he wraps them in his love of Torah, and treats them with respect.

"He is a learned man but being humble he carries his knowledge lightly so that it is no burden to him, nor to those he teaches. He seeks no recompense for teaching, stating that he gives nothing of his own, serving only as a portal through which the ancient truths pass on the way to young and eager minds."

"Then why…?"

"It is not his piety we question, Lord, only his melody."

And the Lord said, "So be it. Mr. Mayberg's chants and prayers will remain earthbound until, in his time, he joins us here. Such davening as his they need below, to draw a smile of recognition from a fellow Jew, to linger in the synagogue, extending My Sabbath by a precious moment, gladdening the souls of those who hear him."

And so it is that when Mr. Mayberg davens, the prayers dawdle. In time this pious man will leave us. And then, Mr. Choir Leader, you will be astonished. You will hear harmony and melody such as you never imagined. But not yet. For now, when Mr. Mayberg reads Torah, the pleasure is ours. Ours and God's.

Choir of the Whole

IN SYNAGOGUE ON SATURDAY, Jerry Fischbein turned to me and said, "You should be in the choir." I was expecting it. He says it to me every Saturday when we are both in synagogue. Other people make similar remarks. I have a strong voice and like to sing. I'm very modest in accepting praise, but I usually contrive to sit near Jerry Fischbein when I'm at services.

"Me?" I protest. "I can't read notes. I couldn't possibly sing in the choir. I'd rather be in the choir of the whole, right here in my seat."

I've always loved music though no one in my family played an instrument or could afford lessons. My father had a loud sonorous snore, but no other musical talent. My mother sang a small repertoire of songs about various animals who went to sea, or a-courting, or had their tails cut off.

I sang some of those same songs and some others in and around our apartment in Brooklyn, loud enough to get Mrs. Tannenbaum to shout down to me from upstairs-front.

"Be quiet! You'll wake Mac. He worked all night driving his cab."

And Mr. Tannenbaum, with last night's unlit cigar already clenched in his teeth, awakened not by me but by his wife's unmusical screams, would sometimes join me in a chorus of "Mr. Froggy Went A-Courtin.'"

It is not quite true that I have had no musical training. I took one voice lesson when I was a graduate student at the University of Iowa. Rose Powers, the wife of another student, was studying opera. She heard me sing at a party and encouraged me to take lessons from her own teacher. The teacher was petite and quite beautiful. Before she would allow me to sing a note she told me I had to learn how to breathe. To teach me, she had me lie on her kitchen table with my legs dangling over the end, while she leaned over me and pressed forcefully with her lovely, perfect, small hands, first on my abdomen and then my chest, instructing me to breathe. From the diaphragm. To feel the air flowing in, filling my lungs. Breathe. Breathe. For the next several evenings I dutifully practiced, putting a book on my chest as she had instructed, but breathing at home didn't have nearly the same charms as it did under her touch on her kitchen table. The magic of her hands didn't transfer to the books, and my breathing was uninspired. I gave it up. My musical education was over.

But still I sing, most vigorously in the synagogue. There are prayers that are just right for my range and when those come up in the service I can hear my own voice soaring over the congregation and it sounds rich and thrilling. Sometimes I can hardly contain myself. I want to thrust my voice higher and stronger and further until it engulfs the entire sanctuary, and I feel I could do it, if only I dared let my voice go free.

I haven't always been confined to the choir of the whole. After I graduated from the University of Iowa I took my first teaching job in Fargo, North Dakota, and we joined the local (Reform) synagogue. Eileen taught in the Sunday school. We became friends with the new cantor. She heard me sing and when the High Holy Days approached, she invited me to join her in singing the Kol Nidre, the ancient chant that introduces the Yom Kippur service. It was to be chanted three times, first by her, then by me, and finally by the congregation. Every cantor relishes the Kol Nidre. Congregants who attend synagogue only once a year come to hear that majestic piece of liturgy and expect to be deeply moved by it, expect to hear the gates of heaven creak open when it is sung. I was awed at the prospect but agreed to do it. I chose to sing without the organ. When I was growing up, musical instruments were not allowed in synagogue during High Holy Days services, I explained. The real reason was that I didn't know how to sing with an accompanist.

For weeks I listened to recordings by Jan Peerce, Yossele Rosenblatt, and other great cantors. The more I listened, the more my heart sank. I couldn't begin to sing as they did. They alternated between soaring power and heartrending sweetness, slipping effortlessly into falsetto, then climbing Jacob's ladder to reach high notes that would have shaken the Tower of Babel.

On the eve of Yom Kippur, the synagogue was packed. The rabbi introduced the Kol Nidre and the congregation was quiet, shimmering with anticipation. The Day of Atonement was to be formally ushered in. The cantor sang from the pulpit in front of the congregation accompanied by the organ and a choir. She had a lovely and melodic voice. Then I sang from the back of the balcony, in partial darkness. I could hear the congregants turning in their seats. In my head Yossele Rosenblatt and Jan Peerce sang along with me. I came to the sweet, delicate section in the middle, the section where in my recordings both Rosenblatt and Peerce gave way to the choir, and then I was on my own and I could hear my voice caressing the words, and I knew it was good. For the rest, I am not sure. When I finished and the congregation began the final repetition, my face was hot and flushed and I felt both exhilarated and defeated.

After the services we were invited to the home of the president of the congregation. He publicly thanked me and then said, as if in jest, "I don't suppose we should break the fast so soon, what with the cantor in our midst."

It took me a moment to understand his implication. For him and his guests, the fast was over. I excused myself and we left to continue the fast throughout the evening and the next day. I assume the president served coffee and cake to the guests and that they analyzed the singing and compared it to cantors who had sung at other times in their synagogue. That was always the practice in my wife's house. Her family would dissect every note the cantor had sung and would compare his style to the great ones of the past, arguing about the voice, the technique, the feeling of their favorite cantors.

We left Fargo the next year. Since then, I have sung the Kol Nidre as part of the congregation, the choir of the whole. Sometimes, however, when it is the congregation's turn to chant, I close my eyes and imagine myself in the back of the balcony with no voice but mine imploring God to release us from intemperate vows as we enter into this holy day of awe and repentance. And then I hear my fellow congregants as though they were indeed my choir, and my voice floats above the rest, ascending, ascending. I thrill at the sound and I know, for that moment, that God surely hears and is moved by all of our voices across this vast planet, forming a choir of the whole, entreating for forgiveness and for a year of peace and happiness. And it is good. Very good.

High Holy Days

A Sign upon Your Hands

CANTOR HIRSCH was crestfallen. He awoke one morning just two weeks before Rosh Hashanah, the Jewish New Year, and discovered he could hardly talk. When he attempted to sing, out came a whistle, a wheeze, but no voice.

He rushed to a specialist. "What can I do, doctor?" he asked in a whisper. "I have to be able to sing for the holidays."

"You need to drink liquids, get lots of rest, and most important, give your voice a rest. Don't try to sing. Don't talk. Even whispering is bad. It strains your vocal chords."

The cantor asked anxiously, "For how long? How long will this last?"

"I can't give you a timetable, but it may be weeks."

"But doctor," the cantor croaked, "I…"

The doctor raised a hand and interrupted. "Liquids and rest. And no singing until this clears up, or you could damage your voice permanently. Carry along a pad and a pencil to communicate."

The cantor was distraught. The High Holy Days were the highlight of the year, for him and for the congregation. He had never missed a High Holy Days service, but now it seemed inevitable.

The next day he met with the rabbi. "What did the doctor tell you?" Rabbi Feinberg asked anxiously.

The cantor started to answer, but then remembered the doctor's instructions. He pulled a pad from his pocket and wrote, "Not good. I'm not allowed to talk. I can't sing until this clears up!"

The rabbi said, "That's terrible. For how long?"

"Uncertain," the cantor wrote. "It could be weeks."

The rabbi saw how despondent the cantor was. He took the pad from him and wrote, "Don't worry. We'll figure something out." Then he said, aloud, "Oh, I don't have to write."

They both smiled, and the cantor wiped a tear from his eye. "We'll need to find a substitute," he wrote.

The rabbi agreed. It was already too late to seek another professional cantor. They would have to find a volunteer from among the congregation. Together they generated a list of lay members who might lead the services:

Abe Kauffman. He knows the service inside and out and would be willing, but he would repeat every phrase four or five times, with melodic variations.

Michael Shaw. He recently joined the choir. He has a good voice but has never led a service. Could he handle it himself?

Sara Shaw, Michael's sister. Also a good voice. She studied to be a cantor for a short period. (Will Michael be offended if his sister is asked and not him?)

Israel Markovits. He knows his stuff but he never comes to synagogue any more. He recently married a non-Jewish woman. Should that matter?

Sarah Melzer. She's in the middle of a divorce and getting ready for Jeremy's bar mitzvah. She has enough on her mind deciding how to sign the invitations.

There were other names and more discussion.

They eventually settled on Sara and Michael Shaw. A brother-and-sister team—that would be a winning combination. The cantor wrote an eloquent note imploring each to help out, and after follow-up telephone calls from the rabbi they both agreed. Cantor Hirsch offered to help them plan the service and divide the responsibilities. They would also recruit other members of the congregation for particular prayers.

As the holidays approached, the cantor became increasingly despondent. There was no improvement in his voice and it was now certain that he would have no part in the services. One afternoon, the rabbi was studying Deuteronomy. While reading the passage that is incorporated into the *Shema*, the most familiar prayer in the liturgy, the rabbi suddenly had an exciting new insight into the text: "Therefore, impress these words of Mine upon your heart. *Bind them as a sign upon your hand*, and let them be a reminder above your eyes…"

That's perfect, he thought. "Bind them as a sign upon your hand!" I must speak to the cantor.

Later that day he met with the cantor, and he asked him, "Do I remember correctly that your older sister was born deaf?"

The cantor nodded.

The rabbi asked, "How did you communicate with this sister?"

"We all learned American Sign Language," the cantor wrote.

"That's what I suspected," the rabbi said. "You made 'signs upon your hands,' as it says in Deuteronomy."

He took the cantor's hands in his own and said, "I wonder what it would be like if, for at least part of the services, you were to interpret in sign language while the prayers are being chanted and sung."

Cantor Hirsch glowed. "Oh, Rabbi. What an idea. It could be wonderful. And very beautiful."

And so, on these particular High Holy Days, Cantor Hirsch faced the congregation and though he uttered not a word, he sang brilliantly with his hands and body and face. On Yom Kippur, the Day of Atonement, when the ram's horn was blown for the *tekiah gadola*, the breath-defying final blast, the cantor reached high above his head, spread his arms, opened wide his hands, and there was no person in the synagogue who did not feel the awesome embrace of that final sounding as the fast and the Holy Days came to a magnificent close.

The Men Are Coming

ON MY BLOCK in Brooklyn when evening descended and Yom Kippur was finally coming to a close, one could hear a cry coming from the Jewish homes, as clear and unmistakable as the sound of the shofar itself, proclaiming the end of the fast. It started with Mrs. Reiff, peering out of her first-floor window, and then it was echoed by Mrs. Tannenbaum, above, and Mrs. Namowitz, and Mrs. Goldstein, and Bertha Weinberg, and finally in my apartment: "*The men are coming.*"

And sure enough when I raced out to my front stoop they would be straggling home, wearing dark suits in the warmest weather, clutching their *tallis* bags, coming home after the long fast. On these occasions, Mr. Goldstein would invite my father up to join him, and even me. "Come, it can't hurt, we'll have a little schnapps to greet the new year." And I would toss down the tiny bit of liquid fire Mr. Goldstein poured out for me, raising my glass along with my father and Mr. Goldstein. "*L'Chaim! L'Chaim!*"

I would have been in synagogue earlier that day before coming home at noon for a light lunch. In shul, I sat next to my father, my grandfather, and the neighborhood men. The women, those who weren't at home resting or preparing the evening meal, were in the balcony, behind the *mechitza*. I was surrounded by religious anarchy. The rabbi, wrapped in his great tallis, seemed to be davening only for himself. Various members of the congregation, chanting at their own pace, periodically speeded up or slowed down for a communal response. The service was punctuated regularly by the shammes pointedly looking up to the balcony, pounding on the lectern to shout out, "*Sha! Zol zayn sha!*"—Be quiet!—to no effect at all, while children wandered in and out, upstairs to be with their mothers or grandmothers, downstairs temporarily to seek the lap of a father or grandfather.

There was a mix of piety and levity on the bench where I sat. Lou from across the street used the occasion to trade off-color jokes with Mac Tannenbaum, jokes he had learned on the road. Uncle Joe and Mr. Horowitz discussed the prices of wholesale produce in their respective grocery stores. My father davened conscientiously and in front of him was a man who stood throughout the service, held no book in his hand, and prayed entirely from memory, swaying back and forth, his lips moving quietly. He was blind.

If I arrived at just the right time, I could hear, or better, experience the rabbi's sermon. He seemed incalculably old with his unexpectedly ruddy cheeks and capacious white beard. There were no microphones or air-conditioning in our small synagogue, and I could see the beads of sweat on his forehead as he spoke, but I understood scarcely a word. He spoke in forceful, dramatic Yiddish to which no one around me seemed to be listening. Every now and then, to quiet the hubbub, he was interrupted by the shammes who emitted his signature, "Sha!"

And then, before the Torah service, the shammes's voice became more melodious, more enticing as he auctioned off the various honors: "*Tzen tolah far aliyah sheyni…*"

My father's hand never went up in response to the call. A lack of money was part of the reason, but it was also because my father, a quiet man, could not bring himself to make such a public display. The honors went to others with larger purses and larger egos.

There was a sameness to the holidays in my youth. My father sat in the same place in the synagogue, surrounded by the same neighbors and family. The discussion after the fast was pretty much the same with minor variations: this year the fast was easy/hard; the cantor was in good/terrible voice; the rabbi's speech was inspirational/incomprehensible; the synagogue was too hot/cool; the children were darlings/hellions. On one thing there was agreement: Thank God we made it through another year.

There was generally a sameness to the holidays, but sometimes the unexpected transpired. On this particular Yom Kippur, my father broke his usual habit. He was tired and uncomfortable as the day progressed and instead of spending the day in synagogue, he walked home with me around noon to take a nap before returning for the afternoon and evening service. We hadn't gone far when I spotted something on the sidewalk in front of us.

"Pop," I said, "There's a dollar bill on the sidewalk. Someone must have dropped it." We got closer. "Pop, that's not a dollar, it's a ten!"

We stared at the bill lying on the sidewalk. It was Yom Kippur. We don't handle money on Yom Kippur. But if we left the money there, it would just fly away or it would enrich someone else no more deserving than we. There was no one in sight. We didn't look at each other, only at the bill. A slight breeze caused the corner of the bill to flutter. Instinctively, I reached for it. My father intercepted me.

"No," he said. "You mustn't. In less than a year, you'll be bar mitzvah. It's not right you should handle money today."

"But Pop," I pleaded. "Ten dollars is a lot of money. We can't just walk away. It won't wait for us until the holiday ends."

My father was unyielding. We had to walk on. He wouldn't even let me gently slide the bill toward the edge of the sidewalk with my foot. I looked back with yearning, but we continued on home. When we arrived, neither of us said anything to my mother. Somehow we understood, without discussing it, that this was our secret. My father napped but I kept rehearsing in my mind how I would race back to that same spot while he slept and nab the bill before it was too late. He didn't have to know. It would just have disappeared. It was tantalizingly possible, but I couldn't bring myself to do it, to deceive my father.

When he awoke, I accompanied him back to synagogue for the end of the fast. We took the same route we had earlier when I first noticed the bill and we slowed when we reached the place where it had lain. It was gone. My father could see my agitation and disappointment. He tried to explain that it wouldn't have felt right, that the money would have burned a hole in his pocket and his conscience.

"How could I pray for forgiveness and ask to be sealed in the Book of Life," he said, "if I no sooner stepped out of synagogue than I committed a sin?"

"You could have done something worthwhile with the money," I answered. "You could have gotten something for yourself. You could have gotten an aliyah after all these years."

My father didn't answer at first. "I didn't know that mattered to you," he said.

In truth, I had never thought of it before. It hadn't crossed my mind that he would be chosen for one of the honors, but now, still fretting about the lost money, I said, "Well, sure, it does."

The services had just started when we entered the sanctuary. As usual, the shammes announced the honors for the concluding service: "*Tsen dolar…*" For a moment there were no takers. Then, to my surprise and to the astonishment of the neighbors in our pew, my father raised his hand. He would open the ark for the final prayer. I watched proudly as he stood before the ark. He was shy when he received the congratulations of the rabbi and the other congregants as he stepped down, and then again as we were leaving the synagogue: "Mazel tov, Abe," they said, and he smiled, a little startled at his own audacity.

We took a different route home. My father was silent, immersed in his own thoughts, weary from the long day and perhaps from the excitement of being on the *bima* in front of the entire congregation. He now had to contemplate how he would explain to my mother about the ten dollars he had pledged and where it would come from. But as we approached the stoop of our apartment house he perked up, straightened his shoulders, and walked with just the hint of a swagger as we caught up with Mr. Goldstein and heard the women calling out, "*The men are coming!*"

Hanukkah

HANUKKAH

Hillel and Shammai:
A Modern Spin
on an Old Story

THE TALMUD RECORDS many disputes between Rabbi Hillel and Rabbi Shammai. One of the best known is the disagreement concerning the proper way that the candles should be lit during the eight days of Hanukkah. Rabbi Shammai ruled that eight candles plus the shammes should be lit the first night and that one candle should be subtracted each succeeding night until, finally, there would be only a single candle and the shammes. In that way, the holiday would be introduced in a blaze of glory and would gradually diminish with the passing of each day.

Rabbi Hillel demurred. He argued that just as we should strive to magnify God's name, we should magnify the splendor of the holiday by gradually increasing the symbols of joy and triumph with each succeeding day, ending with all the candles ablaze on the eighth night. As we all know, Rabbi Hillel's opinion prevailed and, to this day, we increase the number of candles each evening.

In most of the disputes between Hillel and Shammai, Hillel's opinion was ultimately adopted. However, in fairness, there is a little-known debate in which Shammai's opinion won out, and it too involves Hanukkah. The dispute was whether the Halacha requires that the right hand always be used to spin the dreidle. In this instance, it was Rabbi Hillel who was the most inflexible. He insisted that the dreidle must be spun with the right hand because when God redeemed us from Egypt with wonders and an outstretched hand, it is clear from the Haggadah that God used His right hand. Similarly, from biblical descriptions, Hillel had deduced that Aaron held the magical staff in his right hand when confronting Pharaoh. Furthermore, most compellingly, the Torah and all sacred Hebrew books are read from right to left, thereby giving pride of place to the right. For all these reasons and more, Hillel asserted, the dreidle is spun with the right hand.

Shammai disagreed. His opinion was based on scholarship and logic, but it must also be acknowledged that his eldest son was left-handed. When this son had tried to spin the dreidle with his right hand, he had begun to stutter and so had to abandon the attempt.

Shammai suggested that it seemed quite likely that God was ambidextrous, meting out blessings and curses with both hands. For, as Abraham Yehoshua Heshel of Apt said (as reported by Martin Buber), "When a man is merciful and renders loving help he assists in shaping God's right hand. And when a man fights the battle of God and crushes evil, he assists in shaping God's left hand."

Furthermore, although Moses carried the first set of tablets in his right hand, the new tablets were under his left arm when he descended from the mountain the second time, because a shard from the first tablets had punctured the skin of his right hand when he flung them to the ground.

Rabbi Shammai also said that although we know that God created Eve from Adam's rib, the text does not tell us which rib, or which side. This vagueness is intentional. From this the rabbis concluded that when a man argues with his wife, a friend should not choose sides but should instead work toward *shalom bayet*—making peace between them. Shammai also pointed out that there was one group of pious Qumran Jews who always read the Torah while standing on their heads so that their blood, the essence of life, would rush to their tongues as they uttered words of Torah, and that allowed them to read from left to right although the text was written from right to left.

The disagreement between Hillel and Shammai was paralyzing for the community and until it was resolved the children were not given dreidles at all during Hanukkah. Finally the unhappy children protested and their unhappy parents protested and it was decided to convene a *bet din* in which Hillel and Shammai would present arguments and a decision would be rendered.

The first to speak was Hillel. He proceeded in a calm and logical manner. "Let us summarize the differences between us," Hillel said. "On the one hand, Rabbi Shammai thinks that it doesn't matter which hand is used in spinning the dreidle. If we follow his logic, we introduce a dangerous precedent, a slippery slope." The members of the bet din listened attentively and several nodded in agreement.

Rabbi Hillel continued. "On the other hand…" he said, and then he stopped abruptly. As soon as his own words, "On the one hand… and on the other hand…" came out of his mouth, he realized that Shammai was right. If it could be on one hand or the other hand, that must mean that either hand will do. The important thing, he realized, is to observe the holiday with reverence and joy.

Hillel smiled when he realized he was defeated by his own words. He graciously embraced his former adversary, and, hand in hand, they left together to light candles, eat latkes, and challenge each other in a game of dreidle. As they were leaving, Hillel said, "Your story of the Qumran Jews standing on their head reminds me of the time I had to recite the entire Torah while standing on one foot."

"Which foot," Shammai asked? But Hillel couldn't remember and it really didn't matter. The Torah, they agreed, can stand on its own and God, in mercy and in justice, is always evenhanded.

There were many other disputes between the schools of Hillel and Shammai, and though in each instance one argument eventually prevailed, the Talmud teaches us that the words spoken by both sides were words of Torah because they were spoken in search of truth. There may be other versions of the story of how Shammai bested Hillel about the proper way to play with the dreidle, but this is the true one. All others are just spin.

How Many Candles?

ZACH AND ALLI were visiting their grandmother and grandfather in Minneapolis during the winter holiday. Zach is four years old and Alli is seven. They were helping their grandmother get ready for the first night of Hanukkah. They called to their grandmother in the kitchen.

"Come and look, Mae Mae, we've got the candles ready."

"I'll be right there," she answered.

When she came in she saw that Zach and Alli had each set up a Hanukkah menorah with eight candles.

"They look lovely, children, but you have too many candles."

"No, Mae Mae," Allison said, "We have eight candles, one for every night of Hanukkah."

"I know that there are eight nights of Hanukkah," their grandmother said, "but tonight is the first night. We only light one candle tonight."

Zach looked disappointed. "But Mae Mae, why can't we light eight candles every night? It's prettier that way."

His grandmother smiled. "I know it's hard to wait. But that's the right way to light the candles. You have to have patience. Patience is part of the Hanukkah miracle."

Allison said, "We are only going to be here for three more days. Then we have to go back to Colorado. If we wait, we won't ever see all eight candles lit."

"Oh, no," their grandmother said. "Of course you will. You'll light candles when you are home, in Colorado."

"But we want to do it here, with you."

"Yeah, we want to do it here, with you," Zach parroted.

"Children, let's wait until your Bapa and the rest of the family come back from shopping, then we'll all figure something out. Now, come and help me set the table for dinner." The children helped. Allison did what her grandmother did, and Zachary did what Allison did. Soon the table was set with dishes and silverware and glasses and sour cream and apple sauce for the potato latkes that grandmother was preparing for dinner. Zachary and Allison put ice cubes in each of the glasses.

Just when they finished, their mom and dad and grandfather came home. Dad said, "Hey, can I get a hug?" Both children hugged him so hard, they almost knocked him down. They also gave their grandfather a hug, but they were more gentle with him.

"Hello, children" he said. "What have you been doing?"

Allison said, "We've been helping Mae Mae and we set up the Hanukkah candles, but we want to light all eight candles and Mae Mae says we can only light one candle tonight."

"Yeah," Zachary said. "We want to light all the candles every night because we have to go home before the end of Hanukkah."

"Oh, but if you do that, the nights will all be the same," Grandfather said, "and that would get boring. Do you know why we light candles?"

Allison said, "I know. It's because of long ago in the Temple, when the oil lasted eight days instead of just one day." And Zachary added, "Yeah. It was a miracle 'cause there was only enough oil for one day and the lamp kept burning and burning."

"That's right. And on Hanukkah we remind ourselves of the miracle. We make it happen again. Each night we light another candle and that way each night we remember the miracle. That's the tradition."

"But Bapa, we want to see all the candles lit while we're here, with you and Mae Mae," Allison said.

"Yeah, in your house, and then later in our house," Zachary said.

Grandpa said, "I'll tell you what. For tonight, let's just light one candle, as we're supposed to, and I promise that, before you leave, we will have eight candles burning even though it's not the eighth night."

That night and the next two nights, the children each put the correct number of candles in the hanukkiah, and they all said the blessings and played with dreidles, and opened the small gifts their parents and grandparents had given them.

On the fourth night, their last night before going home, Mae Mae reminded Bapa, "You promised the children they could light eight candles, and this is their last night with us. This time tomorrow, they'll be home already."

Grandfather smiled. "I know," he said. "I have a plan."

After dinner, the children gathered for their last evening in Minneapolis. They were sad to be going, but they were also excited. They wondered how Bapa would keep the traditions of the Hanukkah holiday, and also his promise to the children to light all eight candles. All day the children and the adults had been asking him, but he only smiled and said, "You'll see. I have a plan."

Finally, it was time to light candles. Allison prepared her hanukkiah with four candles. Zachary started to put eight in his, but his grandfather stopped him. "Nope. This is the fourth night, Zachary. Just put four candles in the holders."

Zachary started to protest, "But you promised…" His mother told him to wait and see Bapa's plan.

When each child had prepared his candles, Bapa said. "I promised you that tonight we would light eight candles, and we will."

He took Allison's hanukkiah with its four candles, and put it on the table next to Zachary's. Then he moved Zachary's hanukkiah and put it just in front of Allison's so that his four candles covered the empty spaces in Allison's. Then he said to Zachary,

"All right, boychik, you count. How many candles are there?"

The children looked and looked. Then Zachary started to giggle. "There are eight candles. Bapa, that's funny," he said.

And Allison said, "So that was your plan. How did you think of that?"

"It was a miracle," Bapa said, and everyone began to laugh.

"All right, children, now let's say the blessings and light our eight candles."

"Ten candles," Allison said. "Don't forget the shammes." Everyone laughed some more.

"You are right," Bapa said. "It's even a bigger miracle than I planned."

They lit the candles, said the blessings, and looked with pleasure at the dancing lights that reminded them of the miracle that happened long ago. And of the smaller miracles that happen every day of our lives in our homes and in our families.

Elana's Magic Dreidle

THE CHILDREN were visiting their grandparents during Hanukkah. They lit the candles, said the blessings and sang some songs. Then they opened their presents and played dreidle on the living room coffee table, as they always did. Elana's grandfather held the dreidle upside down and tried to spin it on its stem. It took several tries, but he finally made it work.

"Every year I have to practice all over again," he said.

Elana won game after game, until Jacob had no chocolate gelt left. Elana returned all of his chocolate coins—except for the one she had eaten during the game.

"Do you want to play some more?" she asked.

"I've had enough," Jacob said, and he went to his room to count his chocolate gelt and read a good book he had gotten as a present.

Elana and her grandfather continued to play, and again she won every game.

"From now on I'm going to call you the '*Dreidle Meidle*.' How do you do that?" he asked.

"I don't know," Elana answered. "It must be my special dreidle. I got it from a boy in Hebrew school. He came from out of town and none of the other kids wanted to play with him, so I did. At the end of the year he had to go back to Kansas, but he gave me this dreidle as a present. He said it was magic. I know he was kidding but it sure is a great dreidle. I keep winning with it."

The next day Elana was practicing spinning her dreidle on its stem. She heard her grandmother fussing and muttering. "I'm getting old. I just put my eyeglasses down a moment ago and now I can't find them anywhere. You haven't seen them, have you?"

Elana's dreidle was spinning crazily. It almost jumped to the end of the coffee table, and then, quite suddenly, it plopped down. Elana spun it again and it did the same thing, ending in precisely the same place. She walked around the table to where the dreidle was pointing. There, on the couch cushion, were her grandmother's eyeglasses.

"I found them," she called out. "They're right here on the couch."

Her grandmother gave her a big hug. "You're a very clever girl."

"No, I have a very clever dreidle," Elana said.

The next morning her grandfather was doing a crossword puzzle. "I'm stuck," he said. "I need a seven letter word that stands for "giant." I think it ends in *th*.

Elana spun her dreidle. It landed on ג (Gimel). "I don't know the word, Grandpa, but I'll bet it starts with a *G*."

"You're right. It's Goliath! How did you know that?"

"A little dreidle told me."

Grandpa laughed. "That's a good one. A talking dreidle."

"Really, Grandpa. It doesn't talk, but it signals things."

Later, she and Jacob played the dreidle game again, and she kept winning. "You must be cheating," he said.

"No, I'm not," Elana answered.

"Then let me use your dreidle," Jacob said.

He spun it and ש (Shin) appeared. That meant Jacob lost again.

"I quit," Jacob declared. And he left the room.

Her grandfather approached Elana. "What's the matter?"

"It's my dreidle," she said. "I always win, and now nobody wants to play with me." She was almost in tears. "What's the good of magic if it makes everyone else angry?"

"Why don't you just use another dreidle?"

"I tried that, Grandpa, but all the dreidles are somehow together on this. No matter what I do, I always win."

"I think your magic dreidle is a little *fardreit*. Maybe we should consult with a doctor."

"What kind of a doctor works with dreidles?"

"A spin doctor."

"Grandpa, this is not a time for jokes. This is serious."

"OK, we'll have to manage this ourselves. You said that your dreidle gives you signals. Can you also send signals back?"

"I don't know, Grandpa. I never tried that."

"Try now. Concentrate on telling your dreidle that you don't want it to do any more magic."

Elana and her grandfather sat across from each other at the coffee table. Elana closed her eyes and concentrated.

"Did you get through?" her grandfather asked.

"I don't know," Elana said. "I can't tell."

"There's one way to find out," her grandfather said. "Let's play."

They started a game and, sure enough, sometimes Elana won and sometimes she lost.

"It worked! It's acting like a normal dreidle now."

Elana was excited. She called to her brother. "Jacob, come and play with me."

"Not me," he said. "I'm not playing with you anymore."

"Please," she pleaded. "Just one more time. You'll see. It will be different."

Jacob spun the dreidle. He got a ‫ש‬ (Shin), and almost quit the game, but Elana got a ‫ש‬ (Shin) too. They kept playing and first one child won and then the other. Elana let out a sigh of great relief. All was back to normal again.

Meanwhile, Grandpa called out, "Does anyone know what happened to the brown sweater I was wearing yesterday?"

Elana spun her dreidle and it landed on ‫ה‬ (Hey). "I think you'll find it on a *H*anger, in the *H*allway, near your *H*at."

"Yep. That's right where it is," Grandpa said.

Elana picked up her dreidle and smiled. "Well, maybe it's not entirely back to normal," she thought, "but Hanukkah is supposed to be about miracles," and she carefully put her dreidle away for that year.

Purim

PURIM

Invisible Costume

YEAR AFTER YEAR Robert came to the Purim carnival in the most outrageous costume imaginable. One year he was dressed like a giant bird covered with green feathers, with a long yellow beak that hid his beard, and a cap that came to a point with little bobbly balls on top of his bald head. Another year he dressed as a very large woman, puffed out where such women puff out, with a blond wig and black nylon hose. "The Bearded Lady," they called him that year. Once he colored his beard orange and painted his face green and sang a silly song about ripe and unripe tomatoes. Afterward he broke out in a rash that lasted for two weeks. He loved to think up a disguise that would fool people, especially people who knew him well. Robert began planning his Purim costume months in advance. He kept a book in which he recorded not only his own costume, but all of the other people's costumes as well. He had to be original, the best.

As Purim approached this year, none of his ideas seemed expansive or creative enough. He looked through his notebook recalling previous triumphs, but he couldn't think of anything to compete with costumes he had already used. The more he contemplated, the more anxious he became and soon he was close to panic. Purim would come and he would have no costume. He might as well go to the carnival naked! For one desperate moment he even considered shedding his clothes, but no, after all it was in a synagogue, and he did have to live with the people afterward.

The days passed and Robert spent more and more time obsessing about his costume. Every idea that came to his mind he rejected as being too silly, or obvious, or too much like something he had done in the past. He became sick with worry. His wife scolded him.

"Robert, you're crazy and you're driving me crazy. Eat something. Go for a walk. Do something, only forget about that costume."

Robert left the house. His wife was right, but she didn't understand. Robert was ordinarily a quiet man, but on Purim he became a prince among revelers. As he wandered the streets, musing in this way, Robert passed through a neighborhood along Nicollet Avenue he had not visited for some years, with old buildings, decrepit stores, pawnshops. He paused in front of a store window garishly decorated with designs of animals, insects, birds, hearts. The sign said: "Painless Tattoos. Choose from our limitless selections or design your own."

Robert was fascinated with what he saw and for a moment he considered it. Tattoos all over his body depicting mystical Jewish symbols, lions standing on their hind feet, the serpent, signs of the zodiac. He could wear a toga and a wreath around his head. He started toward the door, when he was seized with fear. "How could I think of going into that awful place?"

He shuddered at what he had almost done and hurried back to his own neighborhood, tugging nervously at his beard, muttering to himself. "There must be limits to what a person will do. Still, every day Purim gets closer and all I can do is pull my beard and scratch my head. All I can do is…"

Suddenly, he had an inspiration. His face lit up with a huge smile. "Of course. I know exactly what I'll do. Why was I so concerned? Tattoos, feh! Especially when a solution is so close at hand. I'm getting a little dippy in my old age. That was a close call; a close shave." He laughed to himself. "A harebrained idea, that's what they'll call it, but who cares." He laughed again.

The night of the Purim celebration, Robert was nowhere in sight. He wasn't in the sanctuary. He wasn't in the social hall. Incredible. He had never missed before. People remarked at his absence.

"Poor old Robert. Must have gone over the bend. Couldn't think of a spectacular costume, and so didn't bother to come."

"There was always something crazy about his obsession with his costume."

"True, but it was a treat to see what he'd think of. I'm disappointed. I look forward to his craziness every Purim."

Just then a stranger approached Harry, one of the old-timers, and commented, "Nice synagogue you've got here. I'm new myself in town."

His voice was gruff and unnatural. Harry stared at him.

"Something wrong?" the stranger asked, and adjusted his cap. Actually, a little more than his cap. His hair slid a bit to a side as well. A toupee.

Harry didn't know what to make of this stranger. The new fellow seemed to enjoy his puzzlement. He stared Harry full in the face, lifted his hand as though to tug at his beard, and then came up empty-handed and chuckled.

"Don't you know me?" he asked gleefully, now in his ordinary voice.

"Well no, I don't think we've...Robert!" the other exclaimed. "Is it you? I didn't recognize you. Your beard, what happened to your beard? You couldn't..."

Robert couldn't contain himself. A success. His biggest success yet. No one had recognized him. He turned to Harry.

"I could. I could. I did. You can't imagine what I almost could. So, no Bearded Lady this year, eh? Tell the truth. You had no idea it was me."

Harry was speechless. Meanwhile a small crowd gathered around, remarking on Robert's new appearance, remembering they had passed this "stranger" without even a nod just moments before.

"Where did you get the hairpiece?" one asked him.

"Don't ask. From my brother. He wouldn't like me to tell," Robert gushed.

Robert was in heaven. All was ecstasy. This was the most marvelous Purim of all. But even as the admirers surrounded him and remarked on his transformation, Robert's mind had already begun racing. After a triumph like this, what could he possibly do next year? Where would his next inspiration come from? He sighed, and then brightened. Borrowed troubles he didn't need. For now, life was delicious. Time to go in and hear the Megillah. Next year, the Lord would provide, as he always had. And he stroked his beard—or thought to, and then laughed as his hand came up empty.

Purim Shpiel

THERE IS ALWAYS a carnival on Purim. Your synagogue and my synagogue will have a carnival. Your adorable children and our adorable children will dress up in costumes and makeup and parade around the synagogue while the parents and grandparents beam and *kvell*. There will be soldiers holding spears and many Esthers and Hamans. But one of the most important persons will be missing. No one will dress up as Queen Vashti. She is the forgotten person in the Purim story. She makes a brief entrance—or lack of an entrance, and then, poof, she is gone, and her fate is unknown. Did she go back into the harem? Did she take a fancy to Esther and coach her so that Esther would be chosen to replace her as queen? Did she cheer when Haman was brought to his own gallows? Nobody seems to care. It is shameful that Vashti has been ignored over all these millennia. There should be a holiday in her honor. Children should be let out of school on *Yom Ha Vashti*—the day she lost her crown (or was it her head?). We should have a Vashti fan club.

Just a little reflection will show that Vashti is a true heroine of the Purim story. Without a rebellious Vashti, there would not have been a Queen Esther. Think of how our history would have changed if Vashti had acquiesced when her no-goodnik husband (it shouldn't happen to any of our daughters) ordered her to entertain his drunken cronies. She might have decided that public humiliation was part of her job and that it would be better to accept the king's command rather than risk her life. If she had made that choice, if she had been a "dutiful wife," there would have been no occasion for the beauty contest that brought Esther out of obscurity and to the king's attention. The king wouldn't have known she existed.

Further, when Mordecai learned that two of the king's servants, Bigthan and Teresh, were plotting to kill Ahashuerus, there would have been no one he could tell. Esther wouldn't have had the king's ear—or any other part of his anatomy. Perhaps the plot to assassinate King Ahashuerus would have been successful and Haman might have taken the king's place. Esther would not have been there to thwart Haman's evil plans.

The Megillah records that Vashti was a beauty. King Ahashuerus ordered her to come to the palace so that he could display her as a symbol of his wealth and power. To him, she was just an object, a trophy. Vashti, at her peril, refused to demean herself by consorting with a bunch of drunken *shikkers*. Besides, she was about to take a nap and she believed in a woman's right to snooze.

She was not only beautiful, she was also a feminist, possibly the first feminist. The king's chauvinistic, white, male, eunuch advisers became agitated when they heard that she had disobeyed him. "Punish her!" they clamored, lest, by her example, she incite all the wives of the kingdom to "despise their husbands…and there will be no end of scorn and provocation." She had ideas about women's rights that were two or three thousand years ahead of their time, and for this she was reviled and banished.

The Megillah doesn't tell us what happened to Vashti after her fall from power. Nor is she mentioned in the midrashic literature. I had hopes the mystery would be cleared up in the Dead Sea Scrolls, but there is no mention of the Purim story in any of the scrolls. In fact, it was only recently that we obtained authoritative information about her, when a new and exciting archeological object was discovered, quite by accident, in Iran.

Many of the younger people in Iran were protesting against the severe strictures of Islamic rule, and the reigning Ayatollah feared a rebellion. To entertain and divert the population, he commanded a group of Palestinian musicians to stage an outdoor rock concert—actually, a rock-throwing concert in which the musicians played melodies by bouncing rocks off trucks, automobiles, school buses, "unfaithful" wives, children's belt buckles, and dental retainers.

By coincidence, Shmuel, a wealthy Israeli adventurer, was just then traveling in Iran under a false passport. He had taken up biblical archeology as a hobby and was making explorations in Iran disguised as a camel salesman. He heard about the concert and immediately made plans to go. His boots were scuffed and dirty, however, so he went to a Shushan parlor to get them polished. When the proprietor found out that his customer had an interest in archeology, his eyes lit up. He too was an amateur archeologist and had found an object he was quite eager to sell if he could get a good price. It was ancient, he said. Very, very ancient.

Into the back room they went and, to his amazement, Shmuel was soon gazing at a very old urn that still had miniscule traces of a substance in it that looked and tasted like cornflakes. Carbon dating would later reveal that the contents and the container were more than two thousand years old.

The exterior surface of the urn was elaborately engraved and decorated with a remarkable likeness of Queen Vashti, wearing her crown, dressed as a lion tamer, cracking a whip over a cowering beast with the body of a donkey and the face of Ahashuerus. Shmuel barely made out a phrase engraved below the picture in an ancient script. It said, "Wheaties Breakfast of Champions Athlete of the Year: 486 BCE." Clearly, after leaving the palace, Vashti had achieved distinction in a new and highly successful career.

We may conclude from this amazing discovery that God did not forget Vashti, although an ungrateful Jewish nation did. We are the descendants of those ancient Jews of Shushan, and it is our responsibility and our privilege to redress this historical oversight. It is in our power to give Vashti the recognition and the *koved* she deserves. She should be accorded a place of honor among the other righteous gentile women who have served our people, like Pharaoh's daughter who discovered Moses, or the Egyptian midwives, Shiphrah and Puah, who defied Pharaoh and spared the Hebrew children, or Rahab, the Canaanite woman who sheltered and comforted the men sent by Joshua to spy out the land.

At this year's Purim carnival, dress at least one of your adorable children or grandchildren to honor Vashti, the fallen queen who made it possible for the Jews of Shushan to survive, and for all of us to have the joyous celebration of Purim even to this day.

Passover

Passover Preparations

THE YEAR AFTER my father died, in 1966, my mother traveled from Brooklyn to Minneapolis to be with us for Passover, a pilgrimage she made for the next thirty years. That first year she came alone. The next year she was accompanied by her sister, my aunt Esther, and my uncle Joe. A routine developed. During each visit the elders took the whole family out for dinner before Passover began. On one occasion we all went to Murray's, a famous restaurant in downtown Minneapolis. We scanned the menu, gasped at the prices, but were reassured that we could have whatever we wished. After Eileen and I and the children had ordered, it was my mother's turn.

"I'll have the salmon, but nothing on the fish. No sauce of any kind. I don't like anything on it. And a plain salad. No onions and no dressing. And the coffee should be very hot. With cream."

"All right, dear," the waitress said.

Aunt Esther gave her order and then it was up to Uncle Joe.

"What will you have?" the waitress asked my uncle.

Aunt Esther answered, "He'll have the fish."

"What kind of dressing on your salad?" the waitress asked Joe.

"He doesn't want dressing. He'll have it plain," Esther answered.

"Potatoes?" the waitress asked, looking at Joe.

"Baked," Esther answered for him.

The waitress finally turned away from Joe and asked Esther, "Will the poor dear want anything to drink?"

Wherever we went, Uncle Joe would walk between the two women. "My two wives," he good-naturedly commented.

When Uncle Joe died, Esther and my mother came alone. They stayed for a week, always arriving on a Wednesday and leaving the following Wednesday, always on the same flight. On a few occasions we took our seder on the road because I was on sabbatical. That brought my mother and aunt to Lawrence, Kansas, and Santa Barbara, California. Wherever our children were, they would return to Minneapolis to be with us and my mother and aunt during Passover.

My mother had special dishes she always prepared for the holiday: coleslaw, sweet-and-sour prunes, and popovers. Her prune recipe has earned international fame. She starts with "sour prunes" that she brings from Brooklyn because we can't find the right kind in the Twin Cities. She stuffs these with pieces of walnut; then she prepares thin slices of oranges and lemons, with the skin still on, makes a sweet-sour glaze, and cooks it all. People at our seders rave about it and I know at least two families who now make it a part of their own seders in Israel. She stopped making popovers after she poured too much oil into the pan and smoke came pouring out of the oven. We could never prevail on her to try again.

One year we became anxious about my mother's health. She had hardly gotten off the airplane when she complained of pain in her right arm. Our daughter, Karen, sprang into action. This could be the beginning of a heart attack, she reminded us. We drove to the clinic and anxiously waited for some indication of what the problem was. The doctor examined her and finally asked, "Did you do anything unusual before getting here?"

"No, nothing," my mother said. "I just rode to the airport with my sister."

"Why don't you tell about the suitcase?" Esther interjected.

"That has nothing to do with this situation," my mother retorted sharply.

"What about the suitcase?" I asked.

"Your mother," Esther said, with triumphant exasperation, "couldn't wait to get help with the bags, so she lugged that heavy suitcase all the way down to the car by herself."

My mother gave her only sister a withering look. The feared heart attack, however, turned out to be a slight muscle strain.

Each year, my mother would have her hearing evaluated at the University Speech and Hearing Clinic in Shevlin Hall, where I worked for thirty-six years until I retired. My mother fussed about these examinations as though she were taking a college entrance test. At our last visit, the audiologist suggested that my mother get a telephone equipped with a volume control. My mother resisted.

"I like my old phone."

"It will help you hear," Dianna said.

"I can hear fine on the telephone," my mother said, "except for my other son who has a mustache and who mumbles."

Dianna tried once more, unsuccessfully, to persuade my mother that a new telephone would help her.

"My dear, when you get my age, you should not have to do what helps you." My mother has educated several generations of young audiologists.

In the early years, we took my mother and Aunt Esther out and around the Twin Cities when they came during Passover. We went to the Como Zoo during one visit. Esther stayed at home to read cookbooks. Aunt Esther doesn't cook very much, but she enjoys cookbooks. She's quite modern in that way.

After walking in and out of many exhibits my weary mother spotted a large stone turtle, placed invitingly in front of one of the buildings, and she decided to rest for a moment. As she sat down, the statue slowly heaved itself up and lumbered a few steps forward before freezing again into immobility. The turtle was old, huge, and alive! My mother's shrieks of terror were joined by those of delight and amusement from my children. That episode is one of our cherished family memories.

On another occasion we explored a new walking path being built along Minnehaha Creek near Lyndale Avenue. On the way back we discovered that there were no steps up the steep incline. We formed a line and the children pushed and tugged my mother up the muddy path to the street, laughing and giggling. These days it would surely be my turn to be pushed and tugged.

My mother came to my retirement celebration in 1997, but didn't have the energy to make two trips the same year and so she missed our seder for the first time and has not been here again. For the past two years she was not in the family picture we take each Passover. She wasn't there to help me carve the turkey and to point out which part I had to save especially for Aunt Esther. We didn't have her special dishes. We didn't have her noodling at the piano, or giving my children the good advice they find it hard to accept from us. Esther didn't come either, and this past fall Aunt Esther died.

Now we are contemplating Passover again, and our family will gather in Minneapolis for at least one seder, but it's not the same without my mother. Of course, we have to be available to our children and grandchildren, just as she and Aunt Esther were all these years. It is important to have that connection. With all of us together, the first Pesach in Egypt doesn't seem impossibly long ago. We can feel our history stretching behind us.

To tell the truth, we are getting a little weary from all of the preparations, and the cleaning, and the cooking for so many people on Passover. Soon the children will have to take over the annual seders. It is time to pass the flame, or the matzos, or the afikomen. But last year we bought a new dining room table that can accommodate more people, just in case. Sensible? You be the judge.

Finding the Afikomen

EVERYONE HAD EATEN and drunk until they thought they might burst, but still the seder meal was not over because they had not tasted the afikomen, the middle piece of matzah set aside at the beginning of the seder as a reminder of the miracle of the Passover. The meal couldn't end and the seder couldn't continue until everyone ate a small piece of the afikomen. But Grandpa could not find the afikomen when he looked for it. It had disappeared, just as it had disappeared last year, and the year before, and every year he had been having a seder for his children and grandchildren.

"OK," Grandpa said. "Who's got the afikomen? Whoever gives it to me gets a prize!"

"I do," said Jacob. "What's the prize?"

"Well, first I have to examine it," said Grandpa. "How do I know it's the real afikomen?"

Uncle Josh chimed in with a loud voice, "Don't give it to him, Jake. You better see the prize first."

"I promise you, it's a nice prize. You'll like it. Just hand over the afikomen so we can finish the seder."

Now his mother, Michelle, chimed in. "What about Allison and Elana and Zach? Don't give it to Grandpa, Jake, until he promises prizes for them too."

Jake was holding the afikomen tightly. He didn't know to whom he should listen.

Grandpa said, "All right. It just so happens I have prizes for all of the children. You don't think I'd forget the others, do you?"

Jake was just about to give the afikomen, all wrapped in a nice cloth, to his grandfather, but David, his father, said, "Wait a minute,

Grandpa, Jake isn't giving you the afikomen until you tell us more about the prize."

Jake pulled the afikomen back from Grandpa's outstretched hand.

Grandpa looked disappointed. He almost had the afikomen and now it was gone again. He thought for a while. Then he said, "How about if I give each of the children a mitten?"

"One mitten?" Grandma said. "What can they each do with one mitten?"

"They can share," Grandpa answered. "It's good for children to learn to share."

All the grownups started protesting at once. "No way." "Uh, uh." "No deal." "That's no prize."

"I have another idea," Grandpa said. "If you give me the afikomen now, I'll give each child a brand-new, shiny penny."

"A penny! C'mon, Pops," Joshua said. "We used to get dollars when we were kids."

"Sure, that's why I can only afford pennies now," Grandpa said.

All the grownups protested again. "Boo! Boo!"

Grandpa said, "All right. All right. There's no need to get excited. You want a dollar, I'll give you a dollar."

Jacob again started to hand the wrapped afikomen to his grandfather, but his Aunt Karen stopped him. "Wait a minute, Dad. Do you mean one dollar for everyone, or everyone gets a dollar?"

"Don't get me confused because you finished your PhD," Grandpa said. "I'm offering a dollar for all the children. They can share. I told you, children should learn to share."

"Pooh!" said Karen. "That's cheap. Don't give it to him, Jake."

Grandpa said, "Then you tell me what you want for the afikomen, Jake. But I want to hear from Jake, not everyone else."

"We're his consultants," Uncle Matt said. "We're like his lawyers."

Grandpa looked around. The room seemed to be full of lawyers. Besides those present, he remembered lawyers from the past, when he was the one clutching the afikomen, and his grandfather was bargaining with him. He remembered his own father, and Uncle Joe, and Uncle Abe, and Uncle Meyer, and Seymour, and his grandmother and mother, and all the aunts who were in and out of the kitchen, all advising him, telling him not to settle for too little, all offering to be his consultants.

"C'mon. Cough up. Make it worth the child's while," he heard them say, the ones who were there and those who weren't.

"All right. All right. Here's my final offer. Each child gets two shiny Kennedy half-dollars. And a big kiss. But Josh, don't put your hand out. Twenty-six years old is not still a child."

Everyone sat back at the table, the afikomen was passed around, and each person had a piece. Grandpa showed how his grandfather used to nibble it into the shape of an olive. They sang more songs and soon it was time to go home. Grandpa gave all the children—even the big ones, the kiss he had promised, and they all put on their coats and said goodbye and went home to sleep.

A little later Grandpa was helping to clean up. He cleared the table and brought dishes into the kitchen. When he picked up the Haggadah where Jake had been sitting, he saw something shiny. It was the two Kennedy half-dollars Jake had earned for finding the afikomen. Jake had left them behind.

Pass the Bread, Please

DURING PASSOVER, Andrew visited his neighbors, the Siegels. Andrew is not Jewish.

Mrs. Siegel said, "Are you hungry, Andrew? Would you like a snack?"

"Oh, yes. I would love a snack," said Andrew.

Mrs. Siegel brought out some things to eat. Gefilte fish, potato kugel, and charoseth left over from the seder.

Andrew looked at the fish. "What's this?"

"It's gefilte fish," Mrs. Siegel told him. "Try some. It's good."

Andrew wrinkled his nose. "It doesn't look like fish. I go fishing with my dad and I never caught a fish like that." He pushed the plate away.

"Well, then, try something else. How about some charoseth? It's really good. It has nuts and apples. Even a little wine."

Andrew looked interested. "Wine? My mother doesn't let me drink any wine. I'll have some of that 'gross-it' stuff."

Mrs. Siegel laughed. "Not 'gross-it,' Andrew, 'charoseth.'"

Andrew tasted the charoseth. He liked it. He asked for more.

Mrs. Siegel said, "We eat charoseth at our seder, Andrew. We put it between two pieces of matzah and make a sandwich."

That seemed like a good idea to Andrew. "I want to try it in a sandwich too. Pass the bread, please."

"We don't eat bread during Passover, Andrew. Only matzah," Mrs. Siegel told him.

"Why not?" Andrew asked.

"During Passover Jews don't eat bread, because many, many years ago we were slaves in Egypt, and when we were freed we had to leave very quickly, and didn't have time to let the dough rise to bake bread."

When Andrew came home, his mother asked, "Did you have a nice time at the Siegels'?"

"Pretty good. I ate some 'gross-it' with wine in it! But it didn't make me dizzy. And I found out that Jews don't eat bread on Passover because they used to be in a hurry. But there's something I can't figure out."

"What's that, dear?" his mother asked.

"How come they're still in a hurry during Passover?"

Andrew's mother smiled. "That's a good question, Andrew. You'll have to ask the Siegels sometime. Maybe after Passover, when they're not in such a hurry."

More Maror

ELANA ROSE AROSE, wriggled her toes, and put on her clothes the morning of the first seder. She was visiting her grandparents. Elana lives in Maine, but she had come to Minneapolis with her family so she could help to "seder" Four Questions. ("That's an awful joke, Grandpa.")

Her grandmother was preparing the bitter herbs for the seder plate and her eyes were tearing. Elana said, "Why are you crying, Grandma? Are you sad?"

Her grandmother said, "How could I be unhappy when you are here with me on such a special holiday. But I do feel a little sorry for the horseradish. The poor thing has been scraped, grated, and mashed. It doesn't look at all like itself."

"Don't feel sad for the radish, Grandma. Everyone will remark on how nicely it clears their sinuses. And Grandpa will tell about the time David tricked his non-Jewish friend into eating a whole mouthful, and his eyes began tearing, and he turned as red as a beet, and everyone laughed, even the friend when he finally stopped coughing and choking."

Elana's grandfather heard what she had said, and he smiled. "Elana, maybe you should lead our seder tonight."

"Oh no, Grandpa, you lead it. I'll just correct you when you make mistakes."

Elana's grandmother added some beet juice to the grated horseradish and now it did look very tempting and innocent. You couldn't tell how lethal it was until you had some on the tip of your tongue.

That evening the family gathered for the first seder. David had brought another non-Jewish friend, Eric, who had never been to a seder. Grandpa took some parsley and said, "Now we'll do the *karpas*, and we'll dip the first of the bitter herbs. Who knows why we dip parsley into salt water?"

"I know," Elana said. "The salt water reminds us of the tears we shed when we were slaves in Egypt and we had to work hard and we suffered. But the parsley reminds us of spring and that we should be happy now because we are free."

"That's the Passover story," Grandpa said. "We start the evening remembering bitterness, but we end in joy and happiness, especially after your grandmother serves the chicken soup." He passed some of the parsley to everyone and told them to dip it into the salt water, and to think of how wonderful it is to be free, and how tears can turn into happiness. "Now, everybody dip and we'll say the blessing."

Later—it seemed much later—it was time for the *maror*. Everyone could smell the soup steaming in the kitchen, but first the middle matzah was broken, the afikomen was hidden, and some of the matzah was eaten with the horseradish that Grandma had prepared.

Everyone watched expectantly while Eric heaped the lovely looking horseradish onto the matzah. "This looks good," Eric said. "Why is it called maror?"

"You'll understand in a minute," David said.

Eric ate the maror and the matzah in one gulp, and, to everyone's amazement, he didn't blink. Instead, he said, "That was good, Is it proper to have more maror?" He saw everyone looking at him. "Did I do something wrong?"

"No," David said. "But we were wondering whether you found that just a little bit tangy."

"Sure," said Eric, "but it's nothing compared to lutefisk."

Elijah's Cup

THE DINING ROOM TABLE was set with the special dishes and the fancy tablecloth that Grandma used only on Pesach. When the seder began, each person at the table had a kiddush cup, even the children. There was a kiddush cup in the middle of the table, too. It was the prettiest of them all. Allison, almost five years old, noticed it just when her grandfather said, "Allison, are you ready to ask the Four Questions?"

Instead of answering, Allison asked her grandfather, "Bapa, who is that cup for?"

"That's Elijah's cup. We'll come to that later in the seder. Now it's time to ask the Four Questions."

"Who is Elijah? Is he coming to our seder?"

"Of course. Elijah comes to everybody's seder. But not until later. Now we have to hear the Four Questions."

Allison looked puzzled. "How can he go to everyone's seder, all at the same time?"

"It's a miracle," Grandpa said. "And do you want to know another miracle?"

"Sure," Allison said.

"Well, another miracle is your grandmother's matzah-ball soup. But if we don't hear the Four Questions soon, we'll never get to that miracle."

Allison said, "Bapa, don't joke. I want to know about Elijah."

"Answer her, Dad," Allison's mother said. "We are supposed to ask questions at the seder."

Grandfather said, "But 'seder' means order, and that question is out of order."

Allison's father interjected, "We told the children to ask lots of questions at the seder, not just the Four Questions."

Grandfather said, "All right, Allison, I'll tell you about Elijah. He lived a long time ago. He was a great Jewish prophet."

"What's a prophet, Bapa?"

"A wise and good man who had a message from God. He told everyone that God wants us to help poor and sick people. Now his spirit visits every seder, and even though we can't see him, he sips the wine that's left for him in a special cup, like the one in the middle of our table. It's called Elijah's Cup."

"When will he come?" Allison asked.

"Later in the seder we'll open the door for Elijah and invite him in. You can be the one who opens the door."

"And that's when he sips the wine?" Allison wanted to know.

"Yes. That's when he takes a sip of wine. You look carefully at the cup, and you'll see that a little bit is gone after we invite Elijah in."

"Allison thought for a while. "Couldn't we invite him for the whole seder, Bapa? I could make room for him next to me."

"Oh, but he has so many seders to visit, Allison, it wouldn't be fair to keep him here all night."

Allison nodded. She was thinking about Elijah and his special cup.

Her grandfather said, "Any more questions, Allison?

"Yes," Allison answered. Then she asked the Four Questions in Hebrew. Everyone was very proud of her.

Later, Allison opened the door for Elijah. When she returned to her place, she could see that a little of the wine in Elijah's cup was gone. Uncle Josh, who was sitting right there, was sure she was right. He smiled and said he saw the wine go down with his own two eyes.

Everyone laughed, including three-year-old Zachary, because he liked to laugh when the other people did. Allison thought she heard Elijah laughing too, but it was hard to tell with all the noise.

"Next year," she thought to herself, "I'm going to listen and watch very carefully."

Where Is Elijah?

ORDINARILY, ON THE eve of Passover, Elijah prepares for his marathon trek around the globe by studying the Heavenly Rolodex to be sure he has not missed any addresses or changes of address where Jews will be congregating for the first seder. Then, it is his practice to take a few moments before departing to greet his heavenly neighbors with a wish for a happy and kosher Pesach. And always he saves his warmest greeting for Moshe Rabbeinu—Moses, our teacher. Sometimes Moses jokes that had the peripatetic Elijah been his guide, it wouldn't have taken him forty years to make it to the Promised Land.

This year was different. In heaven, preparations for the seder were already beginning. The celestial choir could be heard practicing the traditional tunes, and the sages and prophets were having their annual disputation about whose turn it was to ask the Four Questions. Moshe Rabbeinu, who was to lead the seder, was studying the Haggadah. The angel Michael was working on the seating chart. He was the first to notice that something was amiss: The rolodex sat untouched and unattended; the special robes Elijah donned for his journey still hung in his closet. Elijah seemed to have made no preparations for his visit to earth.

It was unthinkable that Elijah would not appear at every Jewish seder this night. The Talmud doesn't even consider whether a seder that isn't visited by Elijah is kosher. Though he can only be sensed and not seen, Elijah is a link between ancient times and the world to come. He especially delights the children and he whispers words in their ears that they don't even know they are hearing, but that fill their hearts with love for their families and for the Jewish people. He is the symbol of deliverance that the Passover celebrates.

When Michael became aware of Elijah's absence, he asked the angels Gabriel, Uriel, and Raphael whether they had seen him any time that day. "No," each answered. No one had seen him. Michael organized a search party but Elijah was nowhere to be found. This was not entirely surprising. Elijah spent little time in the celestial spheres. More often he was somewhere on the earth, dressed as a beggar, giving comfort to the poor, the hungry, the oppressed.

Michael himself descended to earth to look for Elijah. He found him, dressed in soiled and tattered garb, in one of the wealthiest neighborhoods in Jerusalem, stopping passersby and calling out: "Tzedakah for the poor of our holy city! Tzedekah so they too can celebrate this joyous holiday. Give thought to your brothers and sisters in need!"

Some stopped only long enough to jeer. "You are fouling the air, old man; spoiling the holiday spirit. Go back to your hovel." Most hurried past without reaching into their pockets, without looking at this sad relic of a man.

Michael approached Elijah. "Here you are. I've been looking for you. Why do you tarry here, where you are not wanted? Why are you not preparing to visit Jewish homes where children and adults anxiously await your appearance? The hour is late."

"Oh, Michael, I've been trying to shake a few coins from these people so that the poor among them can have enough for a seder, to buy wine, candles, matzos. The poor are so many; I didn't feel I could leave."

Michael said, "Think of the children who look forward with excitement to your entrance; and of the righteous, many of whom have suffered throughout the year, who open their door to you with anticipation and hope. And the poor for whom you grieve, who have so little but who are nonetheless consoled by your visit. How can they endure if you abandon them?"

Just then a shabbily dressed young man stopped and emptied his pockets of the few coins they contained. "I wish I had more to give," he said.

And a wealthy merchant, inspired by this example, also contributed. "I was not always so well-off," he said. "Thank you for reminding me." Others stopped too, some who seemed to have hardly enough for themselves.

"You have seen the worst but also the best of humanity," Michael said. "May the message of this Passover turn all hearts to compassion and generosity. Now, however, you must come. You are awaited, and needed, to bless the homes of Jews everywhere who gather tonight."

"Yes," Elijah agreed, "It is time. And thinking of the children gladdens my heart. Surely they will grow to understand the real meaning of tzedakah."

"I shall greet you yet again before this night is over," the angel Michael said. "Moshe Rabbeinu has given me the honor of filling your cup and opening the door for you at our own seder."

At every home that Elijah visited that night, he encountered the eager faces of the children peering into the darkness as the door was opened. The children knew he was there. They could almost see him as he took a sip of the wine that had been prepared for him. He would have liked to stay longer, but he did not tarry. Moshe Rabbeinu and the others were waiting for him above. He did not want to be late when they opened the door for him.

Passover Reflections

EVERY PASSOVER WE celebrate all kinds of miracles: the burning bush, a staff that turns into a serpent, the plagues that inflict the Egyptians but leave the Jews unharmed, the parting of the Red Sea. We should also remember the small miracles that occur every Passover in our own homes. Here are some miracles that occurred during the Passover season just last year.

The miracle of the house cleaning. With the world pressing in on us as we raced to and from work, did our daily errands, and got the children to their numerous destinations, we managed to empty and scrub the refrigerator, move the couch and vacuum behind the cushions, take apart the stove, drag the Passover dishes down from the attic, stash the ordinary dishes, clean the shelves, and do the shopping, even though we are getting older, much, much older.

The miracle of the table arrangement. We invited twenty people into our home for the first seder. We began to arrange the tables. First we had to wring our hands and announce that it is impossible. Then we got to work. My wife and I moved all the furniture out of the living room. Then we moved the dining room set into the living room. We took the legs off the picnic table, and dragged that into the living room, too. We took chairs from all over the house and placed them around the tables. We didn't like that arrangement. So, we moved away all the chairs. Then, we moved the table again. We relocated the picnic table, and replaced the chairs. To our amazement, we ended up with the same arrangement we hadn't liked in the first place. We sat down for a moment to think it over. We decided that we liked it after all. We found a spot for everyone. But there was one extra place setting, with no one assigned to it. We counted and counted again.

Somehow, we had set for twenty-one. We removed the extra chair and place setting, and miraculously there was lots of room.

The miracle of the seder service. Everyone took a seat and we began. The children didn't squabble or bicker. They were content with their placement at the table. They said the Four Questions together, without arguing about who goes first. I told some jokes to keep the children interested. (How do we know the first son is wise? Because he asks, "Wise this night different from all other nights?") It was contagious. Bad puns were being hurled like matzah balls. The afikomen was stolen and I found it, tipped off by Maya, the youngest child at the seder who didn't quite get the idea of hiding and negotiating. It's the finding that's fun. The children liked their gifts. Afterward, my grandson Jacob told me he wants to be funny—like me.

The miracle of the *Shulchan Aruch*. Elana asked for more of the charoseth. Jacob was crazy about the meatballs. The *kneidlach* were perfect. I was clearing away the soup plates and Glen protested. He wanted seconds. The dishes kept coming from all directions. The table was groaning. The people were groaning. Still, we ate. Finally, we distributed the afikomen. The children tried to sculpt it into the shape of an olive with their teeth, as my grandfather had taught me so many years ago.

How is this Passover different from all others? My friend Herb used to have a seder as a child, but he hadn't made his own in decades. Before this last Pesach, he fell in an airport, and struck his head. I visited him at home and brought a box of matzos. On the first day of Pesach, he had a sudden impulse to make his own seder. He found some haggadot that had belonged to his grandfather, and that evening he led a seder with his family. It was so enjoyable, he invited some friends and did it again the second night. God works his miracles in strange ways.

The miracle of the afikomen. This story I heard from Mark Fischer. In a certain family the child who found the afikomen refused to give it up because it wasn't midnight and he remembered the rabbis in B'nai B'rak who studied throughout the night. The child could not be persuaded. Suddenly, there was a momentary power outage, and the child saw that the digital clocks in the house all flashed 12:00. He willingly gave the afikomen to his parents, and the seder was completed. There is no report, but I suspect that Elijah's cup was also drained.

So it is each year. The holiday ambushes us. There is so much to be done, and not enough time to do it in, but it is somehow accomplished. We don't have the *koyikh* (strength), but we find it. The table is set. The guests arrive. The children glow with anticipation. The first cup is raised, and we begin. May our memories of Passover be warm and happy ones, and may the miracles sustain us each year as we prepare to celebrate this wonderful holiday of freedom.

Tips on Conducting a Satisfying and Successful Seder

AS A CHILD growing up in Brooklyn I typically attended two seders each year. The first, guided by my grandfather, was brief, encompassing the kiddush over the first cup of wine, recitation of the Four Questions (in Yiddish and Hebrew), followed by a sumptuous meal prepared by my grandmother, and leading immediately to the complex negotiations concerning the reward for finding the afikomen. Because I had some disposition toward more religious observance, I spent the second seder with our orthodox landlord, Mr. Reiff, and his family. In contrast, Mr. Reiff turned to page one of the Haggadah and kept reading in a toneless, insistent, scratchy voice until he reached the final page, with a brief interlude for the meal, not nearly so savory as my grandmother's.

After I moved to Minnesota and joined Adath Jeshurun Synagogue, I realized that neither of these approaches to the seder would serve our modern, enlightened Jewish family and, like many other parents, I studied and pondered ways to make our seders meaningful and enjoyable for our children. Below are fifteen suggestions for making your own seder more lively based on my experience over the last several decades. I do not choose the number fifteen capriciously. There were fifteen circular steps in the Temple, we celebrate on the fifteenth of Nissan, there are fifteen verses to "Dayenu," and fifteen components from beginning to end of the seder.

1. Prepare your own Haggadah and scramble the pages so that there is general confusion about where anyone is in the service. This should create an atmosphere conducive to asking questions.

2. Invite relatives who have not spoken to each other for decades and seat them next to each other. This will promote the family harmony you have been yearning for.

3. Instead of real matzos, cut out the cardboard pictures of matzos from several boxes and distribute them to the guests. See if anyone notices.

4. Drink the four cups of wine with "an outstretched hand," as written in the Haggadah. This will require that each person at the seder drink from a wine glass held by someone else, preferably the relative he hasn't spoken to in decades, another mechanism for bringing family into greater intimacy.

5. Tell the youngest child to prepare the Four Questions but when it comes time to ask the questions turn to the oldest child instead. This is guaranteed to generate a good deal of animated discussion.

6. Put a dental adhesive in the charoseth to invoke the mortar that was used in making the pyramids.

7. When reciting the plagues, get a supply of real frogs and release them. You can probably do the same with locusts, but that might be excessive.

8. When it is time to recount the story of the exodus from Egypt, tell instead about when you were locked in the bathroom at the Radio City Music Hall in New York. Relate this to the experience of the Israelites in the desert. Ask other people to describe episodes in which they too were locked in a bathroom so that everyone has a sense of participation.

9. Serve manna as the main course at the seder meal. It is *pareve*, will satisfy even the vegans in your group, and requires no preparation. Rabbinic authorities have determined that the manna the Israelites ate in the desert is kosher for Passover.

10. Drill a tiny hole in Elijah's cup so that the wine seeps out during the course of the seder. Drill a tiny hole in the table just below Elijah's cup. Remember to place a glass bowl under the table just below

the hole. Do not move the cup or the bowl during the seder. The children will be awed.

11. Arrange to have a tame bear at the door when you open it for Elijah. This will thrill the children. Arrangements can be made with the Como Zoo and it might even be possible to keep the bear overnight so that it is available for both seders.

12. Announce that because of the high cost of gasoline, there will be no prizes for finding the afikomen this year.

13. Announce that you were kidding and that whichever child finds the afikomen will get five gallons of gasoline.

14. Turn up the temperature in the house to 115 degrees so that everyone can experience the heat of the desert, and remind them that that's how it used to be when you were growing up in Brooklyn, without air-conditioning, but you never complained.

15. Disregard all of the above and revel in the experience of camaraderie, friendship, love, and tradition that the Passover seder invites.

The Four Wise Sons

THE WISE SON ASKS . . . The Wicked Son asks . . . The Simple son asks . . . And the Son-Who-Does-Not-Know-How-To-Ask asks . . .

The four young men were sprawled in various postures in the family room doing homework, reading, listening to music while their parents were out shopping for Passover groceries. The television was on and occasionally one or another glanced at it. The boys were close in age, barely spanning either side of adolescence, and similar in appearance. Clearly, they were brothers.

"Soon we'll have to go through it all again," said Jacob, the oldest, with a touch of irritation.

Jon removed his earphones. "What did you say?"

"I said soon we'll have to go through the Four Sons shtick again, and I'm not looking forward to it."

"Yeah, it does get kind of old."

Jacob continued, "Why do we go through this every year, stuck in a mold, always the same, never allowed to change? Jason is always wise, Jon is simple, I'm always 'wicked,' whatever that's supposed to mean, and Jeremy, who is a pest the rest of the year, suddenly doesn't know enough to ask."

"You're right," said Jeremy. "I mean, I know I'll always be the youngest, but that doesn't mean I'll always be too young to ask. I wish they would let me grow up."

Jason looked up from his book and saw Jacob pull a candy bar from his pocket and toss the wrapper behind the couch. "Hey, don't do that. They'll go nuts if there's *chametz* in this room."

"Oh, come off it. They go through the place with a feather and a fine tooth comb. They'll find it. And if not, it won't hurt anything."

"Well, you surely don't seem to want to change," said his brother.

"Oh, OK." Jacob retrieved the wrapper and put it in his pocket.

"No. Not there either. In the trash."

"Come on, let's not argue," said Jon. "We've got to stick together. This is supposed to be a holiday of freedom, and here we are trapped in the same roles every year."

Jacob said, "You've got it easy. You're simple, so no one expects anything much from you. Whatever you say or do is fine. And if Jeremy says anything that ends with a question mark it's a cause for celebration. You can't blame me for being cynical. I make one remark— I dare to say 'you' instead of 'us,' and I'm threatened with a whack in the teeth. Sometimes I think the old man really intends to do it, too."

"Nah," said Jon. "He wouldn't do that."

"Well, I wish he'd make his point with one of you for once, instead of always me. It's not like I never do anything right. It's just that I say what's on my mind. Really, Jason, you ask about rules and customs; I ask about the service. You make a long speech; I come right to the point. You say '*etchem*' and I say '*l'chem*.' What's the big difference?"

Jeremy began to sing, "You say, 'etchem' and I say 'l'chem'…"

"I'm serious," Jacob said. "This whole business of the Four Sons really annoys me."

Jason looked as though he was going to respond with some smart aleck remark, but he held his tongue. Jon finally broke the silence.

"Maybe, Jacob, it's not just what you say, but how you say it. You always seem impatient, like you've got a chip on your shoulder."

"For goodness' sakes, I'm always the bad guy, year after year. Who wouldn't get impatient? Well, I'm not going to do it. I'm not going to be the wicked son this year. If Pop asks me to read it, I'll refuse. And if he insists, I'll walk away from the table. The rest of you can do what you want."

Jason said, "Don't overreact. It doesn't matter who says what. The important thing is that it's Pesach, and the family should be together. If you want, I'll be the *rasha* this year."

"Would you really do that for me?"

"Sure. Like I said, the important thing is family, especially on Pesach. Besides, that would really freak Pop out. It might be fun—you know, change, the unexpected, see how he reacts."

"I'm shocked. I never would have imagined my wise and exemplary brother taking any pleasure out of messing with Pop," said Jacob.

Again Jason smiled and said nothing.

"I've got an idea," Jon said. "How about if this year none of us is the rasha. Suppose we say that each of us, in his own way, is a Wise Son?"

"That's brilliant," said Jacob. "That's really the point, isn't it? We're individuals, we're different, we don't want to be stereotyped. Jon, you're not so simple after all."

Jon blushed under the compliment. "I don't think we should spring this on Pop. Let's cue him in on what we're planning for the seder."

When their father returned, the brothers gathered around him. Jason took the lead. "Pop, we want to try something different when it comes to the Four Sons in the seder. After all, this night is supposed to be different from all others—even all other seder nights."

"OK," Father said. I'm certainly not so closed-minded as to reject something different out of hand—even an outstretched hand." He smiled at his own joke.

"Great. Here's how we want to do the Four Sons this year. Like always, I'll be the Wise Son and I'll say, 'What is the meaning of the rules, laws and customs which the Eternal our God has commanded us?'"

"Very good, Jason," his father beamed, "but there's nothing different about that."

"Just wait. It gets better. Now the second son. Jacob, you read that."

"The Wise Son asks, 'What is the meaning of this service to you?'"

"Now, Jacob," his father said. "Don't be more contrary than usual. That is not what the text says."

"Sure it is, Pop. I read it just like it says."

"Yes, but you know quite well it is the Wicked Son who speaks those words."

Jacob answered, "But Pop, maybe, just maybe, when I say those words I'm not being wicked. Maybe it's wise to ask what the service means *to you*. After all, you're our model, the authority. I think I've been misunderstood all these years. The Haggadah says I exclude myself, but it could be that I'm merely expressing respect for the opinion of my elders."

"That's a novel interpretation, but I can't imagine the rabbis had it in mind. I don't think they knew about spin and political correctness. Still, it's nice to know you consider me a model. Well, go on, I want to hear how else you intend to mangle the tradition."

Jon read, "The Wise Son asks, 'What is this?'"

Father was becoming agitated. "Now, Jon, you also know that's not the Wise Son. That is the Simple Son speaking."

"Pop, when I say, 'What is this?' that doesn't make me simple. I'm being direct, coming right to the point of the seder, asking an open-ended question. I think that shows that I've gotten a bad rap. In my own way, I'm wise, too."

"What's going on here? Have you all gotten together just to annoy me? Jason, are you part of this too?"

Jason didn't answer immediately. Instead he said, "Let's hear from Jeremy."

Father said, "I hope you're not going to tell me that the Son-Who-Doesn't-Know-How-To-Ask is also wise."

"Sure," Jeremy answered. "Scientists struggle with how to ask the right questions. I learned in school that good questions are more valuable than answers."

Father pondered for a while. "Do you mean to say that all four sons are wise?"

"Maybe there are different ways to show wisdom," Jason said. "But not only that. These same four sons may also be cruel. Take Jeremy, who doesn't ask. That can be devastating. I was at a lecture once. An old guy who used to be famous was invited to give a talk. When he was done, no one raised a hand. No one asked a question. He was crestfallen. I felt awful for him."

The boys were warmed up now, bubbling with ideas.

Jacob said, "And it's not just the words that count. It's how they're said. Jason says I sound irritated when I ask what the seder means to you. If I say it with irritation, then I guess I am acting like a rasha, but if I say it because I really want to know what you think, then I'm not being wicked."

Jon tried to inject, "Hey, it was me who said that about you sounding irritated…"

Jason didn't let him finish. "The point is, Pop, we don't want to be seen as one-dimensional. We are more complex than the Haggadah portrays us."

Father said, "I didn't mean to stereotype you. I thought I was conducting the seder in the spirit of the tradition, but you are right. The Haggadah shouldn't end discussion, it should open it up so that we all get a deeper understanding of what it means to be a Jew. Have you shared any of these revolutionary ideas with your mother?"

Jeremy answered, "No, we haven't. We only thought about all this today."

"I don't know how your mother will respond. At her seders your grandfather started at the beginning of the Haggadah and read through to the end. No omissions, no additions, no flourishes. She may not like these new ideas at all."

"We'll chance it if you will, Pop."

At the seder, when Jeremy had spoken his version of the Simple Son, and Father had read, "This is done because of that which the Eternal did for me when I came forth out of Egypt," the boys looked at their mother. She had been silent throughout the recitation. She stared from one to the other and at her husband.

Finally, she said, "If I had been conducting the seder all these years, I would have come to the same conclusion a long time ago. Of course all my boys are smart, and fine, and with God's help, they'll make their own children feel the same way. Who could say otherwise? But, why does it have to be sons? Why not daughters? You think only sons can be wise?"

From that time on the seders each year were filled with novelty as well as tradition, and lively conversation as well as good food. And Jeremy, who used to be too young to ask, was finally a Wise Son, and he glowed with pride and delight, as did all at the seder table.

Freedom Seder

AVRAM WAS ALMOST ninety when he decided to die. He was disappointed that he wouldn't reach his father's years, ninety-two, but the effort to stay alive was too great. Hinda, his wife of more than sixty years, would miss him, but her rapidly fading memory would buffer the loss. The pity was that he had come so close to freedom. Hinda had sunk increasingly into dementia the past two years and much of his physical and emotional energy had been spent caring for her. First they moved from their home of more than forty years into an assisted living facility, but, as it turned out, there was precious little assistance, and he spent almost every waking hour caring for her needs. She would not stay alone and would not participate in any of the group activities unless he accompanied her. Then she became increasingly forgetful and fragile and had to be moved into an intensive-care facility. Avram remained behind in the apartment and for a short while he was free. He visited her daily but no longer had the constant burden of her care on his own shoulders. He could imagine pursuing his interests—the weekly Bible-study group he so enjoyed, his men's group, personal study with the rabbi—and not feeling guilty or conflicted. He would be able to spend time at his computer, writing, without her resenting being shut out. Freedom.

But it was short-lived. He was not alone for very long before he became ill. He thought at first his problems were emotional, the cumulative effect of watching his wife's mental decay and the effort of helping when his help was not wanted. He found himself hovering over her lest she hurt herself, trying to remain patient with her lapses, her repetitious questions. She had ruled over the kitchen for all the years of their marriage but now she could not be trusted at the stove, could not recall how to make a pot of coffee. He had to hide his frustration as she insisted she could manage without his interference. Even as her memory failed she could smell out his anger. It had been a great strain.

His children prevailed on him to see his doctor and almost immediately he was hospitalized with a serious infection in the lining of his heart that could only be treated with risky surgery. He had to choose between certain death if he did nothing, and the slim possibility of recovery if he could tolerate the procedure and its aftermath. He elected surgery, survived and briefly exulted that he had once again beaten the odds. He had been a survivor all of his life. But medical complications set in and he no longer had the will to fight. He was weak, listless and he could see no future worth struggling for.

Avram's passion in his later years, when I knew him best, was to wrestle with God. He envisioned God as an inner force, a creative life force that shapes our actions and our desires. He insisted that God does not reside in the distant heavens. To discover God and what God wishes of us, we must look within. He was invited to write a short Torah commentary for a local newspaper and he chose that most challenging of biblical stories, the *Akedah*, the binding of Isaac. In Avram's interpretation of the Akedah, God did not command Abraham to sacrifice Isaac. God was silent. It was Abraham's own torment at having banished his firstborn, Ishmael, that was the voice in his head. And, ultimately, it was Abraham's own sense of the holiness of life, and not an angel from God, that stayed his hand.

At the weekly Torah study group Avram was the iconoclast, challenging any reading that suggested divine intervention.

"*V'yomer Adonoy el Moshe…*"—"And God spoke to Moses…"

"Now, wait a minute," Avram interrupted whoever was reading aloud. "You don't really believe that God spoke to Moses. We don't even know if there was a Moses. The Torah was written by men, not by Moses, not by God, men with a wise understanding of human nature who wanted to improve the human condition. They invented God to lend authority to their views."

He was admired for his intellectual acuity, for his love of words, their origins and meanings. But he returned to the same theme over and over and he was impatient with disagreement. He was a doubter who seemed absolutely certain in his doubting. He could not imagine that any thoughtful person truly believed in the God of the Bible.

"Avram," I said to him after one session, "you deride people who claim to believe in a literal God, but you, more than anyone in that group, are obsessed with God."

For more than twenty years, Avram and I were part of a group of men, never more than seven, who met at each other's homes. We shared our frustrations and occasional triumphs and endeavored, with mixed success, to hear each other out and provide support, rather than advice. Avram was frustrated with me at times. He wanted me to be less timid, to confront my demons more directly, not to work so hard at being a "nice guy."

Avram pursued freedom from authority, from the grip of the past, from revealed wisdom, from his own passions. His father had been a brilliant, self-taught scholar of Torah and Talmud who came to Minnesota from the Old Country. For years he owned a grocery store on Minneapolis's North Side, but late in his life, after he was widowed and had retired, he began to teach informally at his home. Young people flocked to this gentle, unassuming elderly man with the thick accent and speech that was hard to understand, his face disfigured by cancer of the jaw. He was admired and loved. When the old man was dying in the hospital, Avram was amazed to see the scores of visitors who came to pay their respects and to be at his bedside. This too was a burden for Avram. He was not capable of that inviting, gentle manner that made his father a revered and beloved figure. Avram was also brilliant, but he was too impatient, too insistent, too restless intellectually to attract acolytes as he reached his father's advanced age. The father had been a courtier; Avram was a warrior. From this comparison, too, he struggled to be free.

One afternoon shortly before his surgery, I had come to visit him at the hospital and arrived just as his granddaughter was leaving. I had never met her, but Avram had talked about her often, as he did about all of his family. When she left I asked whether he had had other visits that day.

"Yes, I've had visitors all week long, not only family members. Rabbi Weinberg was here, and Rabbi Field. I chided Rabbi Field that he finally had time to study Torah with me. And Rabbi Silver came, my daughter's rabbi. And others. I can't remember who they all were. I didn't expect so many people. I didn't think so many would care about me."

After his surgery Avram was transferred from the hospital to a convalescent facility. It was during Passover. The facility was not Jewish and there were no provisions for the holiday. Although Avram was not ritually observant, Passover was the perfect Jewish holiday because it combined study, discussion, and family. But this year Avram would not be at the family seders.

Mark, a mutual friend, decided to surprise him with a bedside seder and invited me to join him. "Let's not say anything until we get there," he said. "If he's up to it, it will give him great pleasure."

We met at the home in the afternoon. Avram was alone in his darkened room, in bed. It took a moment before he was aware of our presence but he brightened when he saw us. "Put on the light," he said, "And help me to sit up."

We helped him into a chair. With a flourish, Mark held up a paper bag and announced, "Tonight is Passover, and on Passover Jews have a seder, and Avram, you are not to be excused from the joy and obligation of this mitzvah just because you are in this place."

Mark reached into his magic bag and brought out matzos, grape juice, charoseth, horseradish, a small container of salt water, and three haggadot. Avram could not tolerate the juice, and so I poured out some root beer for him. Mark made the blessing over the first cup and Avram, who had not been able to eat for several days, took a tentative sip of pop. He succeeded in taking a morsel of matzah, but the charoseth was too much for him.

We had a second sip of "wine," said the blessing, and then put aside the food and the haggadot and talked. We talked about Passover's meaning for each of us. Avram was energized. "Freedom—that is the message of the holiday."

"Yes," I said, "but what is freedom? I'm not sure I know."

"All right," Mark said. "Let's each of us tell what it means to be free and whether we feel free now, at this moment in our lives. I'll start. Right now, as I think of my life, I do feel free. I am free to make choices, to set goals. I may not reach them, and I may make mistakes, but I'm free to choose."

"Not me," I said. "I have too many worries to feel free. I worry about my wife, who has diabetes and other ailments and is still mourning the death of our daughter. I worry about the two grandchildren, who lost their mother. I worry about problems my sons are coping with that I can't rectify. How can I feel free with so much worry and so little control?"

"You have the wrong idea of freedom," Avram said. "Trying to control doesn't make you free. In fact, it is the opposite of freedom. Freedom is a way of thinking, a way of feeling. It's like looking for God in a beautiful sunset or in a rainbow. God isn't in the rainbow. He is in our ability to apprehend and appreciate the rainbow. Freedom is in your mind, not in the world around."

He paused for a moment and we were silent. "Even now," he said, "even in this place where I have so little control over my own body, I can be free—I can choose to be free."

We talked a little while longer. This was the sort of discussion that Avram had always relished, but it was obvious that he was tiring. His voice became weak and he was struggling to stay awake. We embraced. Avram had tears in his eyes. "I love you guys," he said.

Later that evening I participated in a seder at a friend's house. As we went through the rituals my mind was still on our freedom seder of the afternoon. I did not see Avram again. He died not long afterward and his children asked all of us in his men's group to be pallbearers. The coffin was heavy and we had to walk a circuitous path to get to the gravesite but I was glad to be there with the others and to provide this last service to my friend, who, as I imagine, is now sitting at God's side, pressing his view concerning the proper interpretation of the *Akedah*, and arguing directly with God about His existence.

Israel

Israel through the Eyes
of a Washing Machine

I DIDN'T EXPECT when I first traveled to Israel that I would come back with stories about laundry. We arrived in Israel in March, 1976. I was to teach in the School for Communication Disorders on the grounds of Tel Hashomer Hospital, and we hoped to experience life in Israel not as tourists, but as a family, shopping, cleaning, meeting neighbors, going to school—the activities that occur when one truly lives in a place.

In the middle of Tel Hashomer Hospital there was a *shikun,* a stand of 25 four-story apartment buildings clustered together like a grove of trees rising above the low-slung hospital buildings and the labyrinth of sun-beaten, sandy roads. Each building contained sixteen apartments, all built to the same specifications. It was in one of these that we lived during our four-month stay.

The shikun functioned like a small village for the doctors and their families. There was a commons area with a playground and wading pool for the youngest children, a day-care center for preschoolers, basketball courts, shade trees and benches, and a soccer field. There was also a small grocery store that sold olives, cheese, milk, eggs, fresh bread, and vegetables that still retained a trace of the fields on their skins. The shikun lacked only one crucial service: There was no laundry facility. A washing machine was a "personal effect," like one's toothbrush or deodorant. Each family had its own.

Our apartment on the first floor of Building 20 was reserved for temporary tenants. The bland, whitewashed walls were decorated with the splatterings of unfortunate insects that had succumbed to former residents. The living room was fitted with two couches, a bookshelf, a coffee table, and two well-worn chairs. The kitchen contained a stove and refrigerator that had served many families before us, a table and chairs, and the minimum of dishes and table service.

Karen (age fifteen) was given one of the two bedrooms. She had a bed, wardrobe (no closet), and a table. She had room to stack her books, her pictures of friends, her memorabilia, her tiny bottles of perfume, nail polish, and eye shadow. The second bedroom was a combat zone. There we placed Joshua (age ten) and David (age sixteen), separated by piles of toys, books, and dirty clothes that formed a natural barrier between them. Each child had a hospital-issue bed designed for someone approximately five feet tall, adequate for Josh, but not Dave, who had already reached six feet. Eileen and I slept in the living room on two couches, one facing east, the other north. The living room had no door. It was also the discussion room, the coloring room, the reading room, the bounce-the-soccer-ball room, and the passageway to the kitchen.

We had a radio but no television, telephone, or car. We yearned most for a washing machine. At first we washed clothes by hand, kneeling over the bathtub even as our parents and grandparents had done, but they at least had a washing board and, apparently, stronger backs. Then we made a happy discovery. Bus 55 regularly ran between the back gate of the hospital and Rimon. In the town of Rimon there was a Laundromat, complete with washing machines and dryers. We could bring our wash to Rimon, mingle on the bus with ordinary people, patronize a local business. Ugly Americans? Not us. We would be common folk who aired our wash in public.

The walk from our apartment to the bus was considerable. The stop was at the side of a dusty road, unsheltered from the sun, with no place to sit. Each week we stuffed the laundry into two large sacks, slung them over our shoulders, and carried them past the other apartment dwellers, past the shoppers in the grocery, past my students coming to the school, past the curious and amused glances that escorted us all the way to the bus stop. On the bus we mingled with the elderly, the very young, or the lame, most of whom were also carrying odd sized and bulky packages. In Israel, everything, including pets, went on the bus.

Our first visits to the Laundromat were scenes of extravagant gesticulation as the attendant and my wife, who took charge of this negotiation, strove to communicate. Eileen knew little Hebrew, the attendant no English. Without a shared language they pointed, pantomimed, and gestured. It worked. The clothes went into the machine and the money into the cash register.

Visits to the Laundromat took careful timing. In Rimon, the shops opened each morning at seven and closed at seven in the evening. They were also closed during the heat of the day, from one to four o'clock. Except for Tuesdays. On Tuesdays, the stores didn't close until two, but then remained closed for the rest of the day. On Friday, the stores closed early and remained closed over the Sabbath, until Sunday morning. With this time frame in mind, consider the contest. We could not leave until Josh was on the bus that took him to school each morning at eight thirty. Then, if the bags and our feet were not too heavy, we could catch the bus at nine and arrive at nine thirty. Then several variables out of our control would determine our success. How many of the machines would be empty and functioning? Would the part for the second dryer have arrived yet from America? Most important, could both the washing and drying be completed before the one o'clock closing? If our timing was off by no more than minutes, we faced the prospect of a three-hour wait in Rimon, drinking Turkish coffee and watching the busses pass by. Or, we could leave the unfinished laundry, return to Tel Hashomer, and then turn around and come back to Rimon to complete the task. Hardly sensible.

There was another option. We could forgo the drying, trudge home with wet clothes, and hang them from lines on our apartment balcony. It must be understood that if the clothes were heavy when brought to Rimon, they were much heavier when wet. Now the afternoon heat was upon us. The path from the bus to the apartment was long. We were tired. Wet clothes thrown over our backs, we made our way toward the apartment, bodies bent with effort. Once at home, we hung the clothes. We were on the first floor and our clothes dripped harmlessly onto the sand below. The clothes from the fourth, third, and second floors, however, also dripped to the sand, but not until first visiting with whatever hung from our lines. Finally, the hot Mediterranean sun would do its work and the clothes would be dry and folded. All would be well until the first socks, shirts, underwear were tossed to the floor and the process began building for the next week.

Of course, not every week is like the last. During Passover, our laundry day coincided with a *khamsin*, a day of extraordinary heat when the only breezes are searing, dry desert winds that take one's breath away. There is no relief except to sit immobile, without twitching. But, khamsin or no, it was laundry day. We made our trek to the bus stop with sacks that were heavier than usual as the days got warmer. After a hot and uncomfortable ride we arrived at the Laundromat. There we were met by a chilling sight. Posted on the door was a sign that said, "*Segur.*" Closed.

"It can't be," I said. How can it be closed? It's only a quarter to ten. The grocery is open. So is the bakery and the butcher."

"Maybe she's sick. Maybe someone died," my wife reasoned.

"It's no excuse," I said. "Laundromats have to be kept open. Doctors, firemen, police, laundry operators are indispensable. They have to be available."

While I fumed, Eileen went into the butcher shop to see what she could learn.

"It's simple," she told me. "Laundries all over Israel close during Passover. It's a tradition. Everyone knows it, except us."

What more was there to say? Eileen had already shouldered one of the bags and was heading for the bus. I followed suit. At the hospital gate, we began the trek back to our apartment, but this time I got no more than a few feet when I felt a hand on my shoulder. It was the guard, beckoning us back to the checkpoint. He had been shouting at me but I had been too preoccupied to notice.

"What's in the bags?" he asked.

"Laundry," I answered.

"Laundry? On Passover? Where are you bringing laundry on Passover?"

As he became more insistent and suspicious, the little Hebrew I knew vanished. He peppered me with questions: Where did I live, what was I doing in the hospital, what was my work? I could see thoughts forming in his mind. Infiltrators. Terrorists. He waved us to the side, held his gun at the ready and ordered a second guard to investigate the suspicious bags. The guard gingerly put his arm into one of the sacks and came up with a bra and a pair of Karen's flimsy briefs. He blushed. He plunged in again and began to reconnoiter in the depths of the laundry bag. This time he surfaced with smelly mismatched socks and a T-shirt imprinted with Coca-Cola in Hebrew script. He motioned to the first guard. "All right, this is your idea. Now it's your turn to dig in the bags."

The first guard surveyed the situation carefully. He clearly had no desire to put any part of himself into that second laundry bag which had begun to stink in the heat. We found favor in his eyes. No longer were we suspicious plotters smuggling contraband into the hospital. He straightened up, shouldered his weapon, smiled apologetically, and waved us on. We had prevailed. But, of course, we still had the dirty laundry.

During our four months in Israel we traversed the Sinai Desert and visited the City of David, Jericho, Masada, the Dead Sea, the Western Wall, several kibbutzim, the tombs of the ancestors, and much, much more. Were we truly in those wondrous places? Something as mundane as our weekly excursion to Rimon gives a sense of reality to events that too quickly became something I seem to have dreamed rather than experienced. The entry in my mental scrapbook of laundry days makes it all more real and more securely implanted in my memory.

Anna's Recollections

ANNA WORKED AT the School for Communication Disorders in Tel Hashomer, where I taught during my 1976 sabbatical in Israel. When I met her, she was in her late seventies, a survivor of the Holocaust. In her mind, recollections from the past sometimes merged with contemporary events, and the shapes blurred in composite images like the shadows cast by a moving mobile. Anna was an extraordinary storyteller, one of those gifted persons who cannot help but make incidents live again. Not by conscious design, but by irrepressible impulse, Anna's recollections made the events of her life appear in front of my eyes.

First I must tell you the story of how she met her husband. She was living in Russia shortly after being liberated from the camp. She already had plans to go to Israel but was still too weak. Besides, she had an important job in Russia. As young as she was, she could speak nine languages. She served as a contact person to aid the "illegal" immigrants streaming to Israel. Later she would join them. For now, she took every opportunity to learn about the country and to meet Israelis. During one such meeting with a group of Israeli officials she was introduced to an attractive man in the Israeli Ministry of Agriculture. She was barely out of her teens and quite disposed to be impressed. This man was an official from the government she was serving. He came from the land that held her destiny. She wanted to know about the country, the cities, agriculture. He happily answered her questions and made Israel seem even more real and desirable. He was surely a messenger of good tidings.

"And you," she said enthusiastically, "you must tell me about yourself. I know only that you are in agriculture. What is your position? What is your government title?"

He was amused. "I have no title. I am in agriculture. I work on a kibbutz farm."

"Yes, yes. But you are not just a common worker. You surely would not have been sent here if you were a common field worker. What is your official position?"

He smiled mischievously. "My official position? Why didn't you say so? Well, I am a specialist." He leaned toward her, confidingly. "I am a specialist in dishwashing. In my kibbutz I am the head, the sovereign, the premier—the Minister of Dishwashing for the entire community." He bowed with mock formality, and straightened up only to double over with laughter at her consternation.

Anna was crestfallen. Could it be true? Did the country for which she daily risked her neck send dishwashers as official representatives? Even when she told me this story, as she mocked herself, a note of incredulity crept into her voice when she recalled the shock of her discovery.

"He laughed at my discomfort, this High Government Official. Now we both laugh when we think of that first meeting. Well, I was two people then. Maybe three. I had just come from the camps, I was doing a grown woman's work, but I still had a young girl's dreams. I will tell you, he didn't remain a dishwasher long once we were married. When he left the kibbutz he retired from this post and solemnly offered it to me. To my recollection, he hasn't washed a dish since."

The simplest remark might call up the powerful recollections that take refuge in Anna's mind. Once I commented casually about an unexpected meeting with an old friend. Years before, Anna too had had such a meeting. It had occurred after the war when she and her husband were on a diplomatic mission for Israel. They were in Russia during the High Holy Days and she had gone reluctantly to a Moscow synagogue. It was packed with Jews (and who knows who else: secret agents, spies, informers). There was scarcely room to breathe in the women's section and in the crush of the crowd she could no longer reach the exit. She was to spend the day in the synagogue despite herself, an unwilling penitent. Worse yet, she had to remain mute. Her mission required that she pose as a native Israeli who could speak only Hebrew. As she glanced about her she felt someone's gaze. She recognized a woman she had known years before as a child in Poland. The woman, now old, pushed and shoved her way closer to Anna, staring at her all the while. Finally she worked her way close enough to reach out and to put her fingers gingerly on Anna's face, as though testing its reality. Tears filled her eyes and her hands trembled.

"Anna," she muttered in Polish. "If I didn't know she was dead, I would swear this was Anna's face. But Anna died. Gone. Like the rest of them."

Anna forced herself to look uncomprehendingly at the old woman, even to recoil from her touch. The woman stared for another moment and seemed about to reach out again but then was pushed back into the crowd, her head bobbing, her body bent with age, confusion, and the pain of recall. Anna remained frozen, not daring to look as the woman vanished again, leaving Anna to recall things and places and people who were no more.

With Anna, memories tumbled after each other and inevitably led to a story. She recalled another meeting with an old friend whom she had not seen in many years. It was in Prague during the early days when she and her husband traveled extensively for the new Israeli government.

"My husband was busy with official affairs and I had much time to myself. One afternoon I had a flash of recall. Leib. Leib Baranowsky. He had married a Polish girl before the war and they had fled to Prague before disaster overtook the Jews of Poland. He had been studying to be an artist, a painter. Perhaps he had survived and was still here. I thought of trying to reach him, but then debated with myself. It might not do his career any good to be seen with the wife of an Israeli official. He might not appreciate a visitor from his past. Still, he had been a childhood friend and the idea of searching for him became an obsession.

"I found many Baranowskys in the telephone book. The first few calls yielded nothing. Finally, when I had begun to despair, I called a number and simply asked for Leib. There was a pause. Then an exclamation of recognition: 'Anna, is that you? My God, can that be you?'

"I can't tell you how I felt. It was as though he had been waiting for my call and the years had not interceded. We arranged to meet the next day at a café. He was excited and eager. When I arrived at the café, he knew me instantly and embraced me before we had exchanged a word. We stayed there only a moment and then took to the streets where we could talk with less concern.

"Leib wanted to know everything, and about everyone. What had happened to so-and-so? Died, early, in a concentration camp. And so-and-so? Also died in a camp but less fortunately, after much suffering. And Dora? And David? And the old people? And the teachers? And the rabbi? And our brilliant friend Avram? Gone. Some in the ovens. Some by typhoid. Some by starvation. Some in the uprising. Most destroyed in the camps.

"Leib was crushed. Again and again he reached into memory to inquire about the fate of some certain one from our past. Of course he had known of the destruction. But never like this. Never so personally and vividly. Now he knew in a different, more searing way."

Anna paused as though she were done and there was no more to tell, but I urged her on. She told me the rest of the story.

"I saw Leib often in the next months. He insisted we meet every week. He had never been religious and in recent years had stopped thinking of himself as a Jew. His wife never spoke of it. His children had not been Jewishly educated. Now it was important. Every week he came to the Israeli embassy and sat. He sat and ruminated. Some weeks he brought his children and they kept the vigil together. It was as close to prayer as he could come. His wife implored him to stop. They had harmed no one. Why must they now suffer for the evils done by others? Would it lessen the anguish and pain of those unfortunate victims to bring ruin and suffering on himself and his family? I too tried to dissuade him, but he persevered. He would not be moved. It was not for the others but for himself that he came each week to perform this act of expiation.

"In time we had to return to Israel. There had been a brief thaw in relations between Israel and the Soviet bloc, but this passed and we eventually were shut off. I have had no word since. Leib, his wife, his family, they have all vanished. I didn't try to make contact with them. I was afraid it would do them harm."

Anna was pensive, lost in her own thoughts. The question she had asked herself so many times surfaced again. "Did I do right? Was it right for me to search him out and fill his mind with the experiences that have come to haunt my own life? Should I have left him in peace rather than tell him about his friends, his neighbors, his people? He suffered and was transformed, but was it for the good?"

Of course, I couldn't answer Anna. I could only record her stories, a fragment of her stories. There had been a young girl, a high school student named Anna. She had been a brilliant student and had been invited to study medicine in a Polish university, a rare privilege for a Jew. She recalled vividly the dismay of her neighbors when she refused. She was not interested in medicine. How dare she refuse? How would that look for the Jewish community? It was thoughtless and selfish to put her own desires above the needs of the community. Anna remembered that her father had stood by her and defended her right to choose for herself what and where she would study.

She remembered, too, how little difference it made. Such argument and vilification for nothing. Just a few months later they would all be swept away, sealed into the ghetto, awaiting the camps. It was a young, a different Anna to whom all of this had happened. Even as the old woman in the Moscow synagogue had uttered: "If I didn't know she was dead…"

"That old woman, she had good reason to think I was dead. During the last days of the war, the Russians were advancing rapidly and the camp was to be abandoned. Those who were strong enough to walk were pushed out on a death march that would claim most of their lives. There were others, including me, who were too sick and weak to walk.

"The Nazis left us behind to die. Why bother with corpses? But first they stripped off our rags. Dead people have no need of clothes. Then each of us was injected with a drug to finish us off. We were left there, frozen, naked, feverish, and poisoned. No human could have survived. Yet, when the Russians arrived some of us had miraculously held on. I was officially inscribed in the record as dead. And someone did die.

The little Anna who was so brilliant a student, who was her father's joy; that little girl did not survive. She did indeed die in the camp."

The Anna who remained from that experience was a teller of stories that came alive as I listened. In the few months that I knew her she inspired me to laughter and to tears. I asked her once if she would write a book with all of her stories. This caught her interest. Obviously, she had thought about it herself.

"Ah, I could write such a book. The things I have seen and done could fill several books. Yes, someday I may write a book. But not like a journalist who cares only about his story. Did I ever tell you about the newspaperman who wanted to interview me, to write my story?" She was off again, ready to recount a story about writing a story.

"After the Russians liberated the camp we stayed a while to gain strength. The Russians allowed foreign journalists to enter, to see what crimes Hitler had committed and how the Russians had courageously rescued us. One man from America, some big correspondent, but I've forgotten his name—he wanted a story from me. I swore I would have nothing to do with him. It was enough to have lived through it. I wanted to put it behind me, not to rake it over for some foreigner to put in his paper.

"But they have ways, these journalists. First they ask a simple question. They promise they will take only a few minutes. Just a few facts. No personal or painful questions. So, I relaxed a little and before I knew it I was laying my soul bare, describing the camps, spilling out my heart, reliving for him the fear, the pain, the hunger, the torture, the abuse, the wretchedness, the dehumanization that had been our constant experience.

"He wrenched it out of me and scratched it all down in his notebook. Then, when it was done and I was too spent to talk any more, too limp and exhausted, he closed the book—flipped it closed with a self-satisfied gesture (I remember it)—and he put his fountain pen in his shirt pocket with great care. Then he smiled and he said words I can still hear, 'Thank you. That's nice. This will make a great story.'"

Anna's voice was filled with hurt and anger. "Do you understand? A great story! I was stunned. That's what he had in his book. That was the sum of our suffering and our lives. I will always hear his voice. I wanted to lunge at him and tear the book from his hands, but I was too weak. Instead, I collapsed."

After a long silence, Anna said, "Yes, someday I will have to write a book. There is much to tell."

Soil from Israel

"SOIL" IS A CHANGELING word. As a verb it means to make *shmutzik*, to stain, to defile, to anger Mother who warned us not to dirty our new clothes. But when it appears as a noun, "soil" is transformed. Now it refers reverently to the earth, the stuff from which Adam was formed and which will be a final resting place for each of us. We dig and plant in the soil, with no concern for becoming shmutzik, because we coax life out of the soil.

Even more to be revered is soil from Israel, in all of its manifestations. Jacob rested on a rock, and it became a shrine. Moses addressed a rock, and it became a fountain. Joseph sojourned in great ceremony to bury his father's bones with his forebears, and later Moses made a similar, though more protracted, journey to bring Joseph to rest in the soil of Israel. We have seen pictures of immigrants falling to their knees and kissing the ground when first arriving in Israel, and of early pioneers proudly and lovingly filtering the soil through their fingers as they established the first agricultural kibbutzim.

But, it must be admitted, in our day the sacredness of the land is sometimes overlooked or forgotten. I was standing in line at the central bus station in Tel Aviv. In front of me was a man holding a brown paper bag with a generous supply of sunflower seeds. He was passing the time, as do many in Israel, by popping the seeds into his mouth and spitting out the shells while we all waited to board the bus. In front of him was a well-dressed businessman with an attaché case at his side. The sunflower man had a well-practiced rhythm of reaching into the bag, propelling the individual seeds into his mouth, and spraying the shells in front of him. Some fell to the ground, others on the businessman's shoes, and still others on the attaché case.

The businessman moved the case closer to himself, but it was still in range of the shells. Finally, in frustration, he protested.

"Watch what you are doing. You are making a mess on my case and on me as well. Besides, this is the land of our ancestors. You should have more respect."

The sunflower man was not impressed. "My ancestors were never in this bus station, and you are free to move yourself and your brief-case as far as you wish."

It seemed for a moment there would be trouble, but a peacemaker was also in line. He spoke to both of them. To the businessman he said, "There is no need to make a big thing of this. You can move your case." And to the marksman, "It's not necessary for you to spit your shells all over the ground. You can be more considerate."

Blessed is the peacemaker. He ended what was becoming an increasingly ugly confrontation. The sunflower man forgot his former adversary and turned on this intruder to tell him what he thought of his meddling in something that was not his affair. The businessman, sizing up the situation, quietly slipped to the back of the line, leaving the others to finish the argument. Fortunately, the doors to the bus opened just then and in the pushing and shoving to get aboard, the men were separated and the episode was ended. Scattered on the ground were the remains of the seeds, and the sunflower man procured a seat near an open window, still holding his brown bag.

My first experience with soil from Israel was much earlier than this encounter at the bus station, and it was not in Tel Aviv, but on the North Side of Minneapolis. It occurred shortly after my wife and I and our two small children moved into an apartment on Penn Avenue, across from Beth El synagogue in an area that had once been the center of Jewish life in the city. When we arrived in 1961, Jews had already begun to migrate to the suburbs, and the once-thriving Jewish community was in transition. Still, within walking distance from our apartment there were kosher butcher shops, delicatessens, Jewish bakeries, a fresh fish market, Mr. Gold's Variety Store, a scattering of conservative and orthodox synagogues. All of this would vanish in the aftermath of the upheavals of 1967–1968 after Martin Luther

King Jr. was assassinated, but for the two years we lived there, the Minneapolis North Side was warmly reminiscent of the community I had known as a child in New York.

The main thoroughfare was Plymouth Avenue. Soon after we moved in I set out to explore the many storefronts along this busy avenue, and I noticed a rather dingy-looking shoemaker's shop. A few scattered items were on display in the window but what especially caught my attention was a small jar of dirt with a crudely lettered sign: *Soil from Israel.* This was a Jewish shoemaker! I had never met a Jewish shoemaker. In New York, the shoemakers were invariably Italian. I never discovered how he had acquired the soil from Israel, whether he had collected it himself or it had been given to him; whether it represented a memory, or an aspiration. But I did learn that he was a survivor of the Holocaust.

It was almost fifteen years later that, with my family, I made my first trip to Israel, to teach at the School for Communication Disorders in Tel Hashomer, and there I came to know the magic of the land firsthand. For four months my wife and I and our three children lived in a tiny apartment on the hospital grounds and toured as much of the country as my teaching schedule allowed. We searched out relatives in Haifa and Tel Aviv, and a childhood friend who many years ago had made aliyah to kibbutz Urim in the Negev. We vacationed briefly in Arad, visited with new friends and friends of friends, all of whom invited us into their homes. In the last week, we toured the Sinai with the Israeli Society for the Preservation of Nature.

Throughout our stay we collected tiny rocks and soil from the various places we visited. When we returned to Minneapolis in July 1976, just a few days after the dramatic rescue by the Israeli Defense Forces in Entebbe, my wife sorted and labeled the samples according to where they had been collected. We had long since moved from the North Side and into our own home, but like the Plymouth Avenue shoemaker, we displayed our treasures in jars. Now we too had "soil from Israel." As the years passed, we put our Israel picture albums on the shelf among the others we had assembled. The samples of rocks and soil were brought to the basement and became invisible as new memorabilia were accumulated. It would be fourteen years before we returned.

I remembered the collection one day when I was planning a hospital visit to a friend who had become very ill. I knew of Leon's great love for Israel and thought it might cheer him to have a bit of Israel in his hospital room. I rooted around in my basement until I found our Israeli treasures. I filled a plastic pill dispenser with some soil or fragments of rock from various locations in Israel, and labeled each compartment.

On my next visit I carried the pill dispenser in my pocket, prepared to joke about the healing powers of soil from Israel, but when I arrived at Leon's hospital room and saw him surrounded by the paraphernalia of illness I had misgivings. I worried that my gift might seem morbid rather than the expression of my hopes for his recovery. Just before I ended my visit I showed him the pill dispenser and told him what it contained. He put it on his bed stand and assured me that he was glad to have it—that if he couldn't go to Israel just then, he'd be happy to have Israel come to him.

Leon's condition worsened. He died in the hospital just before Yom Kippur, and just after the birth of a grandson. The following evening, after the funeral, relatives, friends, and colleagues crowded into the family home for shivah. When the service was over, one of his sons took me aside and asked, "Do you remember that container of soil from Israel that you gave my father while he was in the hospital?"

"Yes, I do," I answered.

He looked away for a moment and then blurted out, "Was it really from Israel?"

I was puzzled by the question. "Of course. Why do you ask?"

He paused again, and finally said, "I just wanted to be sure. We buried it with him. We placed it in my father's coffin."

THE STORES OWNED by Jewish merchants that I first saw along Plymouth Avenue are long gone. The synagogues too, some converted to churches. The "North Side" exists mostly in the memories and nostalgic stories of the old-timers who once lived there, and in a handful of scholarly publications about its history.

A newcomer to the neighborhood today would have few clues that there was once a vibrant Jewish community along these streets and avenues. There is certainly nothing to testify that a shy Holocaust survivor once operated a shoemaker shop on Plymouth Avenue, or that a touch of the Holy Land inhabited his shop window. I never learned anything about the proprietor, not even his name. He was not young when I first saw him, and it is likely that he too has passed on. If so, I hope that his jar of Soil from Israel, the symbol of pride and hope that first arrested my attention, was returned to the earth with him.

Kfar Menachem

IN KFAR MENACHEM there were generous people. And oranges.
Joshua, our ten-year-old son, will best remember the oranges. They
were so plentiful and accessible, he was incredulous. We first encountered the oranges moments after we met our host, Mayrum Baram.
Mayrum was waiting for us at the end of our long, hot bus ride. We
had barely exchanged names when he ushered us into the kibbutz
dining room and set before us the leftovers he had saved from the
afternoon meal—cold chicken, salad, and some sort of stewed fruit.
Josh found little of this to his liking, but later, on the way to the Baram
home, we passed a sight that caused his eyes to widen with wonder.
Along the path he spotted a large wooden crate, big enough to climb
in, stocked with a rich treasure. It was filled with oranges.

Josh asked, with studied casualness, "Whose are those oranges?"

He was answered in good English by Amazia, son of the Barams.
"They are anybody's. They are for anyone who wants them."

"What I mean," Josh said cautiously, "is who owns all those
oranges in that big crate?"

"And what I mean," said Amazia, "is that these are our oranges,
grown on our own trees, and put here for the people. Anyone can
have them."

Joshua leaned over the edge of the crate and peered in. So many
oranges. He nonchalantly reached in, found an orange, discarded it,
and selected one he fancied more. Then, just as casually, he stuffed a
second orange into his pocket. He paused for a moment. There was no
reproving word. Now, with more abandon, Josh selected still another
and looked Mayrum full in the face. He found nothing more ominous

there than a smile. He was about to explore further when he heard, "Joshua, enough!"—but it came from me and not from Amazia.

We made our way to the Baram home where we met Roska. There was a stillness in both Mayrum and Roska. One sensed in them enormous strength and resolve. Their faces had been well seasoned by years of coaxing the land to yield and the kibbutz to survive and grow. We soon learned that there was also something more recent, a tragedy that caused their speech to be touched by sadness.

We came to kibbutz Kfar Menachem by way of Adath Jeshurun Synagogue in Minneapolis. Cantor Kula had entrusted us to deliver a gift and a letter to his cousins, the Barams. He assured us we would be doing a mitzvah and that the letter would be a passport to the kibbutz. He was correct. Soon after I contacted them to tell them that we carried greetings, they wrote and invited us to visit. I was slow to take up their offer and one day we received an emissary from the kibbutz. He had come to Tel Hashomer Hospital for treatment and knew we were living on the hospital grounds. He needed to catch the bus back to the kibbutz, but he dared not return, he told us, until we agreed on a date for our visit.

"Perhaps the weekend of Memorial and Independence Days, May 5 and 6," I suggested.

"Perfect. You will find it interesting to see how we celebrate on the kibbutz. I'm sure the Barams will agree."

So it was that Eileen and I and the children, David, Karen, and Josh, were now crowded into the Baram living room while Roska served fresh fruit and juice. We soon understood their sorrow. Roska opened the first of several albums and haltingly, almost apologetically, she explained that these contained pictures, and letters, and the history of her son. Not of Amazia, but of a younger son who had been killed in the Yom Kippur War of 1973. The albums chronicled the short span of his life—standing beside his sister, frolicking with Amazia, dressed in his new uniform, competing in sports, smiling winsomely on his birthday.

Roska told the story behind each picture in hushed tones. She recounted stories, childhood pranks, matter-of-fact observations of no special consequence—the memories to which uncontainable love becomes attached when there is no longer a person to receive it. The books were replaced and Mayrum brought out a collection of beautiful metal Hanukkah menorahs. The son had been born on Hanukkah and Mayrum had crafted each of them with great skill and delicacy. These were the vessels into which he poured his sorrow and love.

The shadows began to lengthen and Amazia announced that it was time for the memorial service. Would we like to come? We need not, if we preferred. Yes, we would attend. Roska, Mayrum, and Amazia led us to a garden area that was lush with beautiful plants and flowers. There were six graves arranged in a horizontal row. Small clusters of people stood silently around each of the graves. After an interval, Roska quietly busied herself with the ferns and plants that framed her son's grave. She and Mayrum watered the plants and carefully rearranged the flowers, wordlessly, and with great concentration. Roska placed new cuttings on the grave, some that she had collected earlier in the afternoon while taking us on a tour of the kibbutz. Even then she was thinking ahead to this moment. Similar activity took place at the other graves. We stood back and observed. Amazia pointed out a woman at the far end of the row, attending to two graves.

"She lost two sons," he whispered, "on the same day. First they brought the news of one, then of the other."

There were no prayers, no Kaddish was recited, and yet it was a prayerful moment. After standing silently and surveying their work, the mourners left to participate in another ceremony that would mark the end of these solemn observances and would usher in the beginning of Independence Day. The entire kibbutz gathered in a large amphitheater. Fires, flares, and a rifle salute signaled that Memorial Day was supplanted by Independence, mourning by celebration, grieving by hope and affirmation.

After the ceremony there was a special banquet, and dancing and treats for the children. Roska and Mayrum could not bring themselves to join the celebrating, but they took pleasure in seeing that Joshua had a full share of treats and that David and Karen joined the dancers. Still later, past midnight, they vacated their home to make it available to us.

"But you mustn't," we protested. "Where will you sleep?"

"It's no trouble," they assured us. "We have a place, much better than many we've slept in." We later learned that they had slept on blankets beneath the kibbutz shower house while we occupied their beds.

The following day we accompanied Roska and Mayrum to a picnic and then a tour of the countryside in a rented bus. One of the members, a former Irgun soldier, explained the battles that had been fought, where the lines had been drawn, where settlements had been destroyed or had endured, in all of the wars since 1948.

It was time for us to return to Tel Hashomer. While the rest of us packed, Josh made one last pilgrimage to the shrine of the oranges and came back with his arms full.

"Is that all you can carry?" Roska asked. "You must also have some for your journey home. Have you a container?" I emptied a canvas book bag imprinted with "Hillel," and Roska stuffed it with oranges and grapefruits. Josh noticed a crack of light and rushed to stuff it still further. The bag was so full of happiness it could hardly be carried.

We said goodbye to Roska and Mayrum, and Amazia got us to the bus stop. We squeezed aboard with our luggage, already feeling tired and hot though the long ride had just begun. We lapsed into private reveries until Josh suddenly sat bolt upright.

"We have to go back," he exclaimed.

"Why? What's the matter?"

"I left my bag of oranges in Amazia's car."

Joshua mounted argument after argument as to why we absolutely had to leave the bus and return to the kibbutz and we tried to convince him the bus could not go back. He finally ceased fretting only when he became exhausted and fell asleep. We woke him at Tel Aviv to catch the next bus. He said no more but remained morose for the rest of the trip and for days to follow.

Several days later we had a note from Amazia.

Dear Mr. and Mrs. Siegel,

I would like you to know that your stay with us was a great pleasure to us. For my parents it was a great relief. Last year it was very difficult for them and I realized that your presence was a blessed gift. They didn't think so much about the tragedy, and being with you filled the day with something pleasant and refreshing

All the best and au revoir.
Amazia

One afternoon not long after, we returned from a trip and found a package in front of our door. It was filled with oranges and grapefruits. Josh could not contain his excitement and joy. They were sent, as Mayrum's note indicated, "so that your lovely Josh won't be disappointed." The Hillel bag was not there. They had accepted it as a memento from us.

I contemplated how little I had understood about those few days we had spent with the Baram family at Kfar Menachem. It had seemed to me that we had brought nothing to them but a thirst from the bus ride and an appetite for new experiences. We had not realized we would be standing at the edge of their sorrow, and I feared that we had appeared at a difficult time—that we had inadvertently run roughshod over their grief. Instead, our presence was "a blessed gift." I was glad and grateful that our intrusion into their life had been welcome.

Josh, on the other hand, was not weighed down with these philosophical deliberations. He too was grateful and glad but in a much more immediate and practical way. He celebrated the occasion by munching on the fruit, fully convinced that the world is, after all, just, magnanimous, and very juicy.

The Road to Masada

AHMAD HAD GENTLE WAYS and gentle eyes, but in the darkened taxi I could only sense them behind me as we sped along a narrow, uneven road, bumping and jostling. We were packed into the cab. My wife, our three children, and Ahmad were in the back. I sat alongside the driver in the front seat. I peered out of the windows, straining to make some sense of the countryside, but all I could see were the headlights bouncing off the darkness as the car kept plunging recklessly forward. After the first excitement of piling into the taxicab and squabbling over seats, the children had fallen silent. We were heading toward Masada from the city of Arad at four o'clock in the morning so that we would see the sunrise and make the long hike up the serpentine trail before being caught up in the heat of the day.

I had come to Israel for a four-month sabbatical at the Chaim Sheba Medical Center in Tel Hashomer. In the past week, Tel Hashomer had turned oppressively hot, and so we had arranged a few days of vacation in Arad to get a reprieve from the stifling air and to bring some relief to our son David, who was suffering from asthma. David was sixteen. Ahmad could not have been much older and the two formed a quick friendship over a Ping-Pong table when we first arrived. Karen, our fifteen-year-old daughter, hovered at the edge of the friendship, and ten-year-old Joshua intruded himself into any cluster of two or more.

Ahmad worked at the hotel. He spoke to David and Karen in a combination of English and Hebrew. Whenever he was free, he sought David out for a game of Ping-Pong. He was shy with my wife and me, and spoke to us mostly with smiles and gestures. I was pleased that even in a new country David had so readily found a companion, as he so often did when we vacationed in the United States.

One of the attractions that had drawn us to Arad is that it is close to Masada, and shortly after we checked into the hotel I asked the clerk how we might arrange an excursion. We wanted to visit Herod's fortress and the children wanted to tell their friends they had climbed the famous snake path. The guidebooks made it seem exciting and dangerous. It was especially important that we climb the snake path rather than take the shorter and less arduous Roman path.

Ahmad overheard me questioning the clerk and he enthusiastically offered to make the arrangements for such a trip on the following morning. He had never climbed Masada, he told me, and would be glad to accompany us. If we agreed, he would arrange to have a friend drive us to the mountain and would hike the trail with us.

As we were lurching along the rough, unforgiving road, I tried to get a glimpse of our driver. I could only see a faint profile, as he stared ahead at the road. I couldn't make out any of his features, but his face seemed rough and forbidding. His left hand was wrapped in a white gauze bandage and was supported by a sling around his neck. He drove with his right hand carelessly crossed over the steering wheel at what seemed breakneck speed. I had heard him exchange only a few words with Ahmad in what I took to be Arabic. I don't know whether he understood English.

We were some distance from the hotel, the taxicab already inhaled by the darkness, when I realized that I had been reckless. We were in a taxicab with two Arabs, both strangers. One I had never met before and the other a youth I had known only two days. No one at the hotel had been in the lobby when we left. We had not passed any cars along the way. None of our friends in Tel Hashomer had any idea about this early morning excursion. On other trips we had been with groups of Jewish tourists and invariably accompanied by an armed guard. The guards were often middle-aged reservists who seemed less our protectors than congenial companions, but they carried serious-looking weapons and occasionally showed an unexpected alertness, an arresting quickness.

After we had been in Israel for a short while, we were surprised at how secure we felt and how little we were concerned for the children's safety, even when they walked back from school at midnight from the Lag b'Omer bonfires. In Israel everyone looked out for the children, and we felt entirely safe despite the ominous stories in American newspapers.

There were occasional reminders of danger, however. When we visited Uncle Shmuel in Haifa he had screamed at us in dismay and raced to find our son Joshua, whom we had allowed to wander out of the house in an Arab neighborhood. And in Hebron we had seen Israeli soldiers brandishing weapons at the alert as they patrolled rooftops, and we sensed the sullen resentment of the local Arabs as our tour group walked to and from the buses. In Hebron I was afraid.

Now, pressed together in the isolated taxicab with Ahmad and the rough-looking driver, I was again afraid, but here there were no guards or fellow tourists to look to for reassurance. I realized that we were alone with two strange Arabs and utterly vulnerable to any sort of harm our companions might be contemplating. Perhaps they saw us as enemy Jews, or despised Americans, or Zionists. Perhaps the entire trip had been planned by Ahmad with a dark purpose from the start. I had thoughtlessly and naively put my family in a dangerous situation. Did the children sense the danger too—is that why they had become silent? I dreaded what lay ahead.

Just as my anxiety became oppressive, the unnatural quiet was broken by a loud shriek from the back seat. David had tried to shift Joshua from his own legs onto Karen's. Karen protested vigorously. Joshua responded by bouncing up and down on whomever's knees he was on. David joined the cacophony of protest. Joshua became more energetic. My wife tried to quiet them all with her own loud blast. Ahmad began to chuckle at the chaos and entered the fray. With the silence broken, the daylight also found a crack to penetrate, and we could see the base of the mountain. We had arrived at fabled Masada. I could finally make out the driver's face. He smiled patiently as I paid him. He was tired and obviously relieved to see us depart.

As soon as they were free from the cramped taxicab the children raced for the path. Ahmad, who a short time before had seemed ominous and threatening, was everywhere, shepherding Joshua when he strayed, recovering the camera one of us had left behind, running ahead to be with David and Karen, falling discreetly back from time to time to check on my wife and me, always smiling gently and softly.

To our surprise, we reached the top with no difficulty at all in less than an hour. The driver, out of apparent solicitude, had led us to the Roman rather than the snake path. The children were overcome with disappointment, but Ahmad quickly repaired the situation. He found a comfortable place for my wife and me, surrounded us with snacks and drinks, and then gleefully led the children on a wild chase back down the path so that they could climb again on the formidable snake path. They disappeared from sight in an instant, but I felt not the slightest anxiety, only some small concern that Joshua might drive Ahmad to distraction. We toured the excavation while the children were gone. In a couple of hours they straggled back up the path, and Ahmad now had two heads. Joshua was on his shoulders and had been for most of the climb.

The trek back to Arad was dreary. It turned hot and humid. There was no taxi to take us back and so we were forced to wait a full two hours for the bus. The children occupied themselves with desultory games but they began to wilt as the afternoon wore on. We had had very little sleep. Joshua fell asleep in the bus shelter. Ahmad and the others did some minimal exploring but it was too hot to stay out long in the sun. The bus finally came and deposited us back in Arad. Gratefully we went back to our rooms for naps.

Two days later it was time to return to Tel Hashomer, the children to their schools and me to my teaching. I had exchanged only a few words with Ahmad since our trip to Masada. He had cleared our table in the dining room, but was again shy and reticent. When we left we were, as usual, running late and I had no chance to say good-bye.

That was more than forty years ago, years often filled with harsh conflict between Jews and Arabs in Israel. The Arabs I see now, on television, are glaring at cameras, throwing rocks and bottles in confrontation with Israeli soldiers or settlers. The promise of peace between our two peoples, raised and then shattered again and again, seems painfully remote. And yet, when I think of Ahmad, it is with warmth and gratitude. Ahmad had gentle eyes and gentle ways. That is how he remains fixed in my memory, and that memory is touched with hope.

Other Stories with a Yiddish *Tam* (Flavor)

The Road to Chelm

IN OLDEN DAYS, the wise men of Chelm didn't live in Chelm. They lived in a place called Dorten. The wise men recorded the exact location of Dorten[1] and many other facts about their lives there before they set off on their great migration, but they feared that their secrets might pass into unfriendly hands and so they wrote their records in a special code that nobody could understand, not even the wise men themselves. The records still exist but no one can decipher them. There were no maps and so we no longer know where Dorten is or even if it still exists. But we do know from stories passed on from generation to generation that the trek from Dorten to Chelm was long and difficult.

The story of the arduous journey is retold by the elders of Chelm each year during Purim. One summer a great drought overtook Dorten. The rains didn't come in their season and the farmers' crops withered in the ground. The sun burned so hot that the cows gave milk that turned into sour cottage cheese the moment it felt the air, and the chickens laid hard-boiled eggs with shells so thick you couldn't crack them with a hammer. The streams and the ponds dried up and there was neither food nor drink. The residents of Dorten were desperate.

Jacob, their leader, called an emergency meeting. He said, "Something must be done or we won't survive the summer." The wise men applauded this very wise observation and then fell silent. After a long pause, one of them said, "But what should we do?" This question was followed by another long pause. Another of the wise men sighed and said, "We must do something." This very good suggestion was followed by more applause, and more silence.

---

[1] "Dorten," in Yiddish, means elsewhere, over there, far away, not here.

Finally, Jacob said, "I have a plan." Everyone listened eagerly to hear the plan, ready to criticize it as soon as he was finished.

"This is summer," Jacob said, "and what comes after summer?"

"Fall," one of the men answered tentatively.

"Exactly," said Jacob. "And what happens in the fall?"

"The leaves fall, the temperature falls, and the blessed rain falls," said Shmuel.

"Exactly," said Jacob. "So, all we need to do is to wait until fall."

Shmuel said, "Yes, but if we wait for fall, we will die of thirst and hunger." There was no more applause, only loud and sorrowful sighs.

After thinking about this for a while Jacob said, "Well, my brothers, if we can't wait for fall to find us, we must go to find fall."

"But where is it?" one of the men said. "How do we get there?"

"I am not sure," Jacob said, "but I'm certain we will recognize it when we see it."

The next morning, all the residents of Dorten loaded their belongings on carts, and wagons, and on their backs and set out in the blazing sun to find Fall. They weren't sure which way to go but they knew that Fall was someplace in the future, and the future was always ahead, so they just walked straight ahead, except for when they had to take side roads to get around obstacles, or to avoid robbers, or when they got lost, which was quite often because even the best roads didn't always go straight. They walked and walked for days and days and then weeks and weeks. Soon the days became shorter, the air was cooler, leaves from the trees collected beneath their feet, and it began to rain.

"Just a little bit further," Jacob announced. "I think we are very close."

A short while later, tired and weary from their long trip, they stumbled out of the forest and into a village that looked very much like the one they had left. There they found houses like those they used to live in; and a synagogue like the one they used to pray in; and a meeting hall just like they used to have their meetings in. But the buildings were abandoned. There was not a person in sight. They shouted and called, but no one answered. Only a few stray dogs appeared and seemed remarkably happy to see these strangers.

Jacob said, "Dear friends, I think we have finally found what we were seeking. God has provided this village for us and made it similar to our old home so that we should feel familiar and comfortable."

The weary travelers each selected a home like the one he had lived in before their great journey, and they were joyous to have found so wonderful a town, even better, they thought, than the one they had left.

After they were settled, the wise men gathered in the meeting hall. First they cheered and applauded Jacob, their wise leader, who had brought them to this wonderful new place. One of the men said, "What shall we call our new village?"

Because they had gone out in search of *Fall*, and had traveled so *Far*, one of the wise men suggested they call their new home *Farfallen*.[2] The wise men knew that one should never accept a first suggestion, especially if it was someone else's, and so Farfallen was rejected.

Jacob said, "In this new town, as was true in our old village, the streets are lined with beautiful trees that God has provided for our comfort. Let us name our new home after these trees."

That suggestion was greeted by applause, but none of the men knew the name of the trees, and, being very wise, they were not about to admit it.

Jacob's daughter had come to fetch her father to dinner. When she saw that her father didn't know the name of the tree, she whispered in his ear, "It's an elm tree, Papa." But she had caught a cold on their long journey, and it came out sounding like "chelm tree."

"I remember now," said Jacob, "those are chelm trees."

The wise men all agreed. "Yes, those are chelm trees."

Jacob's daughter smiled but said nothing, and from that day on, their village was called Chelm.

That is how in the olden days the wise men left Dorten and founded Chelm. Occasionally some of the young men or women who have heard of the great pilgrimage have tried to discover the whereabouts of Dorten, but none has ever succeeded. Instead, they have remained in Chelm, where they have written learned books, told their stories, puzzled over their mysterious records, and produced many generations of wise men and women.

---

[2] In Yiddish, "Lost, abandoned, doomed."

Jelly Bread Up,
Jelly Bread Down

SHLOMO WAS AN early riser. There was always much to be done and since it was Shlomo who would be doing it, even more to be undone, and so it was important to get an early start. He awoke each morning with a blessing on his lips for the new day and a prayer that God would grant him the wit to use it well, for although he was a simple man who yearned for a simple life, his days were often hectic.

One bright morning he cut a thick slice of dark bread, heaped it with his favorite jelly, and only then decided to smear it with butter as well. Some jelly slithered off the bread, onto his hands, and then onto his clean shirt. He distractedly ran his fingers through his hair, leaving a sticky trail of butter and jelly. He brushed away a fly that had also come to dine on his bread and jelly and the bread flew from his hand, somersaulted through the air, hung there indecisively, and finally fell to the ground.

When Shlomo stooped to retrieve his breakfast he was startled to find that the bread had fallen with the jelly side up. Shlomo was amazed and perplexed. He didn't know whether to celebrate his good fortune or to tremble that the natural order of his life had been disturbed. He tried to puzzle through the meaning of this extraordinary event. He creased his brow, stroked his beard, waved a finger in the air, and thumped on the table, but to no avail. This was beyond his powers of understanding. He decided to consult someone wiser than himself: the rabbi.

As is always true in such tales, the rabbi was in his study poring over the holy books when Shlomo barged in.

"Rabbi," Shlomo said. "Something strange, something mysterious has happened to me in my own home and I don't know whether to fast or to say a *Shehecheyanu*."

The rabbi was accustomed to Shlomo's misadventures and he reluctantly put aside his book. "Now, now, Shlomo, don't make yourself too excited. Just tell me what happened."

Shlomo thrust the slice of bread, with the fly still buzzing around it, in front of the rabbi. "Just moments ago, Rabbi, this very slice of bread that I am holding in front of you fell from my hand and onto the floor!"

Shlomo waited expectantly for the rabbi to comment on the amazing occurrence, but the rabbi simply said, "Nu. So? Why is that so unusual? It's not the first time."

Shlomo said, "But it is the first time, Rabbi. Look closer. Don't you see what's unusual?"

The rabbi peered at the bread. Except for where Shlomo was holding it, with his thumb immersed in the jelly, there was nothing amiss. The rabbi suddenly understood: On an ordinary day, on a hundred earlier days, the bread would have landed jelly side down and become encrusted with dirt. The bread Shlomo was holding had fallen with the jelly side up. Such things never happened with Shlomo. This was not Shlomo's lot.

"Shlomo, are you saying that this is the very slice of bread that fell to the ground? And are you saying that you did nothing to repair it before bringing it here?"

"Rabbi, I didn't do a thing to it. I brought it right here so you could see what happened. Even the fly is the same one that caused me to drop the bread in the first place."

That evening, after the men of the village had completed their prayers, the rabbi recounted what had happened to Shlomo. At first the men smiled, thinking this would be just another of the many escapades that so often befell poor Shlomo. But when the rabbi concluded dramatically with the words, "And the bread fell with the jelly side up," they clutched at their prayer books and there was a gasp of incomprehension.

"My dear friends," the rabbi said, "I have consulted the sources but find nothing to account for Shlomo's sudden change of fortune. I only hope that it doesn't mean, God forbid, that some dark force is at work in our community."

The men of the congregation stirred uncomfortably, wondering whether their own transgressions might have brought an evil spirit into their midst, but each forgave himself immediately and began to wonder, instead, about the transgressions of his neighbor to the right and to the left. A spirit of suspicion arose and these good men began to murmur against each other.

The rabbi admonished them. "No, no, my brothers. This is no time for dissension. We must join together to discover the meaning of this unusual occurrence. Surely there is a lesson in it for us all."

They pondered, studied, argued, and sought analogies from the sacred texts, but they could not penetrate the mystery. There are many stories of how God has tested men with adversity, but not with good fortune. What could it mean if, suddenly, Shlomo was no longer himself. Could a leopard change its spots? Would day continue to follow night? Would the rains come in their appointed season? Would the holidays and festivals follow each other in the correct order? How could one be sure when celebrating Hanukkah that it wasn't, in fact, Purim?

After an eternity of disputing and discoursing late into the evening and long after the men should have been at home with their families, Shlomo himself, who all this time had been a silent and miserable witness, called out excitedly, "Rabbi. Rabbi. I think I understand what happened. I think I have it figured out."

The elders shushed Shlomo and reminded him, irritably, that he was the source of all this trouble, and that because of him their evening meals were growing cold.

But the rabbi knew that God is partial to simple men and often reveals his mysteries through such vessels as Shlomo. "Speak up, Shlomo," he said. "What do you have in mind?"

Shlomo took a deep breath. "They are right, Rabbi. I'm the one who is at fault. I made a mistake, but I was too foolish to realize it until just now. I was a little hurried this morning and I didn't pay attention, and I had a lot of things on my mind, and I was trying to remember something that I hadn't even forgotten, and I couldn't find my shoes, and…"

"Shlomo, please," the rabbi interrupted. "Get to the point."

"That's where I'm getting, Rabbi. The point is, I was so harried this morning that I smeared the jelly on the wrong side of the bread."

A smile spread over the rabbi's face. The elders sighed with relief. Each thought privately that he was just about to offer the very same explanation before Shlomo jumped in. They silently congratulated themselves on how kind they were to tolerate this simple fellow who didn't even know which side of his bread to jelly.

As for Shlomo, he rejoiced that he had restored peace and comfort to his neighbors and his community. The world seemed right again and he was content in the knowledge that now and always, he was what he was.

Perpetual Care

THE SUMMER I turned sixty I finally determined to have hip-replacement surgery. For some years I'd been in pain, limping noticeably, consuming large quantities of aspirin daily. But it took a signal event, my sixtieth birthday, before I mustered the courage to go ahead with the operation. At the same time I did something else I'd been contemplating for several years. I filled out a living will. Living will. It's really a living *won't*. I won't take this. Don't give me that. I won't eat, I won't drink, I won't breathe—*I won't dance, you can't make me*! (Well, maybe now, with my new hip…)

After the surgery, I spent one week in the hospital recuperating. The nurses, the doctor, my neighbors who visited were all exceedingly attentive. They congratulated me for putting one foot in front of another, for walking up stairs, for putting on my own shoes. I have done little else which has generated such universal approval. That same summer my wife, Eileen, suddenly developed diabetes and was also hospitalized. This I took very badly because it wasn't even her birthday. We had separate vacations, she in Fairview and I in Midway Hospital. We had different diets, too. Intravenous insulin for her, and morphine for me.

Now that I'm past sixty, Eileen wants to move into a town house that requires less care. After thirty years in the same house I finally figured out how to grow crabgrass and now she wants to move. But first we'll get a new furnace, change the fixtures, put in new carpet. We'll make the old place just like we always wanted, and then we'll move into a town house which won't be at all like we always wanted. There's another reason I resist moving. My neighborhood has become young again. The old folks have moved on. Young families with small children now surround us and I can hear the irresistible sounds of children growing, and houses groaning under the strain.

I've also started thinking about a more permanent kind of real estate deal—a long-term investment. To make it more plain, I've been thinking about where to be buried. Eileen and I are both originally New Yorkers. Our immediate families are all still in New York, the ones who are alive and the ones who are dead. The decision is easy for them. They will remain New Yorkers, and not even death will them part. But we've been gone for much longer than we ever lived in New York.

Before settling in Minnesota we lived in New York, Iowa, North Dakota, and Kansas, a new address almost every year. Two of our children, David and Karen, were born in Parsons, a small town in southeast Kansas; the youngest, Josh, in Minneapolis. Since coming to Minneapolis, we've put down roots and lived in the same house—the only house we've ever owned—since 1963. Our children are scattered and mobile. Only David lives in Minneapolis and we don't know how long any of them will stay put. So where should we be buried? Where do we belong?

My father was planful about death. He joined a burial society when he was first married, and secured the only parcel of land he and my mother ever owned. When he died, my mother had a double headstone put up. The right-hand side is engraved with loving words about my father. The left-hand side is blank. On the Jewish holidays my mother visits the cemetery. My cousin Neil brings along his video camera to record the scene. They visit the graves of the many family members buried there, pull out the unwanted growth, clean up the bushes and plants, and place a pebble on the gravestone. Neil recorded an especially poignant moment during a recent visit. It shows my mother, already in her late eighties, gingerly approaching the headstone. She stumbles a bit, and with one hand grasps my father's side of the stone to steady herself. My father is still helping out. She straightens herself up, fixes her hair, and positions herself next to the blank side of the stone so that the writing on my father's side is visible. She slowly turns her profile toward the camera; one hand is still on the gravestone. She is serious, not smiling, but not grim. I can't read her mood. What is she thinking while she poses there, standing slightly off balance and unsteady, trying to look her best, squinting a little in the sun, standing at the entryway to her final resting place?

MY FRIEND HERSHEL had many brushes with death as a child but he would never speak of it. He turned away questions with a joke or a quip. During the war his family escaped the Warsaw Ghetto, and Hershel was hidden in a Catholic orphanage in Russia. At the end of the war, his father, convinced that Hershel had not survived, was searching cemeteries, trying to find his son's burial place. In one such cemetery he asked the caretaker whether Hershel was buried there. Instead, he learned that Hershel was alive, but in a hospital and gravely ill with typhoid fever. Hershel pulled through and the family was reunited.

He married a Polish woman, went to college, then medical school. They lived in Poland, Czechoslovakia, Israel, Chicago, and eventually Minneapolis, where we became neighbors and friends. Hershel learned to fly and dreamed of combining his love of medicine with his love of airplanes, but his dream turned into tragedy. He was piloting two doctors and a technician into a part of Wisconsin where they didn't have medical specialists. A storm blew up and the small airplane went down. It took many tense weeks before the bodies were recovered from a half-frozen lake.

The family had to decide where to bury him. Hershel had no formal religious affiliation and he left no instructions. His four children had been raised Catholic. A Jewish cemetery would be alien to his wife and children, and a Catholic burial would have been an offense to his surviving mother and brother. The family wanted to acknowledge Hershel's identity, as well as their own. After much deliberation they chose nonsectarian Lakewood Cemetery, already hallowed ground (though staunchly Republican Hershel might not have thought so) because Hubert Humphrey is buried there. The family asked for my help, and at my request, the rabbi of my synagogue agreed to officiate at the burial even though he had never met Hershel or the family. He read the Hebrew psalms and Eileen and I joined in the traditional prayer of mourning, the Kaddish, while the children stood mute.

The next evening there was a memorial service at St. Patrick's Church, and the family invited me to share the pulpit with their priest. At the start of the service, when they entered the church, Hershel's children knelt and crossed themselves and for the first time I truly understood that they were not Jewish. There was never any question in my mind that Hershel was Jewish. He told Jewish stories. He had a Jewish wit and social conscience, and a ferocious loyalty to Israel. He voted Republican and he never went to synagogue. Still, he was Jewish. But not the children. Funerals help to make such things clear.

MOSHE IS AN Israeli friend. Most of his father's family was wiped out by the Nazis, but Moshe's Uncle Adam, his father's brother, survived and remained in Poland. Moshe never met his uncle but his father, and later Moshe, kept in touch. Life in Poland was hard. Moshe sent clothes, medicine, and money to his uncle and his wife, whatever he could spare. Adam's wife died and so the uncle was alone. He was always grateful for what he received but occasionally he asked for a little more—for a sick friend.

When it finally became possible for a Jew with an Israeli passport to visit Poland, Moshe eagerly made arrangements to meet his uncle. Moshe was scheduled to be in Germany for a psychology conference. When the conference ended, he and his wife and two of their children would drive to Poland. It would be his first visit since the war. For the children, of course, their first visit ever. They would finally connect with the last surviving member of the family. Several days before he was scheduled to leave Germany, Moshe received word that he had better hurry. The uncle was gravely ill. He gathered up his family, rented a car, and they raced to Poland, but too late. They arrived just in time to say Kaddish at his uncle's funeral.

At the cemetery, Moshe noticed a Polish man standing well behind the Jewish mourners. It was unusual for Poles to attend a Jewish funeral. As the small congregation was dispersing, the man stopped Moshe and spoke to him in Polish.

"My name is Leonard," he said. "And I know who you are. You are the nephew. We are like cousins."

He told Moshe that Adam had been like a father to him and wonderful to his family. After his wife died, Adam had become despondent and ill. He was nursed to health by Leonard's mother, Adele, and eventually lived with her and her children for many years though they didn't marry. Adam was ashamed to tell his brother in Israel he was living with a gentile woman, but many of the gifts he requested were to help this Polish family. Then Adele had herself become ill, and now it was Adam's turn to become nurse. He used the money and medicines sent by Moshe's family to care for her until she died. Not long afterward Adam became ill and now Moshe was at his funeral.

"Would you like to see where my mother is buried?" Leonard asked. The next day the two families gathered in the Polish cemetery and stood, tearfully, in front of Adele's grave. In the space of a few days Moshe had lost an uncle he had never met and an "aunt" whose existence he had not even suspected. He placed a small rock on Adele's gravestone. Leonard asked what it meant.

"We place a stone as a sign that mourners have been here, have paid respect to the dead, and have left behind a bit of their heart."

Leonard picked up a stone and placed it next to Moshe's. "I will do the same for your uncle," he said.

BECAUSE I LIVE so far away, I get to visit my father's grave infrequently. My brother visits more often, sometimes with my mother, sometimes alone. We have "perpetual care" for my father's grave and we will have the same for my mother. My brother has suggested that we make the same arrangement for other members of the family buried there. It's really a bargain. For a few thousand dollars we get a mortgage on eternity. How else can care be arranged? We honor the dead by not bothering them. So, perpetual care.

We are blessed in Minneapolis with more room, more open space than in New York, and so I have not yet put down a reservation on a burial plot. Or perhaps it's because I'm still not entirely decided. I'm keeping my options open in case I get a better offer, but I assume that I will be buried in a Jewish cemetery in Minneapolis. It is here that I have spent most of my adult life and where my children were raised although they may no longer live here. And I too will have perpetual care. Workers will come to the burial site, pull weeds, clean up after a storm, make sure the grave is tended. But they won't place a pebble on the gravestone. That they won't do.

Jurisdictional Dispute

ARTHUR WAS STUBBORN, that was not new. But now, as he talked with Philip over lunch in the faculty lounge, he was also being rather foolish.

Philip tried to reason with him. "You really shouldn't walk into that neighborhood alone, even during the day. That would be downright folly."

Arthur folded and stashed his soiled sandwich bag, took one last sip of tea, and rose to leave. "You are too fearful, Philip, always expecting the worst. I'll be walking only half a block from the train. There is no reason to waste money on a cab."

"Please," Philip said. "Just this once be sensible and listen to me. You are asking for trouble. You can afford to take a cab to the hospital. Miriam will be very happy to have you visit her, but not if she knew you were being foolhardy."

"What Miriam doesn't know won't hurt her."

Philip relented. When Arthur became stubborn, there was no sense arguing.

"All right. I can't do anything with you. If I wasn't tied up this afternoon with committee meetings, I'd come with you. I wish Miriam had chosen to have her car accident in a more tranquil part of the city. Thankfully, she'll be out of there soon. Do you know where the hospital is, and how to get there?"

"Yes, yes. I have instructions. I know which train to take, where to get off, which side of the station to exit, and exactly how to get to the hospital. There is no need to worry."

"All right then, go. And give Miriam my fondest regards. We need her back here. There is no one else who will pick up her class on Maimonides, and the students are getting restive."

Philip had good reason to be concerned. Arthur might be a first-class scholar, but that didn't make him a practical man. His lapses were legendary. He walked out of his door one morning and into a very large tree in his front lawn. He hadn't remembered seeing a tree there before. He made appointments and failed to show up. He arranged a surprise sixtieth birthday party for his wife, became absorbed in a text, and left her at the furniture store where he was supposed to pick her up. The guests in his home, hiding behind doors and couches and squeezed into closets, were poised to shout, "Surprise!" for more than an hour. These past two years, since his wife's death, Arthur seemed even more distracted and forgetful.

This occasion was no exception. He had forgotten the book he was going to read on the way to the hospital and leave with Miriam, but he became engrossed in looking around the train, wondering at the secret lives of the others he saw there, and by the time he peered out of the window he had missed his stop. It took a minute to register. If he were to take the train back he would first have to ride to the next station, go down a flight of stairs, cross over to the other side, go up a flight of stairs, and then wait to take the train back. Too much trouble. He would walk the few extra blocks, though Philip would surely disapprove.

Arthur was caught up in his own thoughts when he emerged from the subway and began walking back toward the hospital. Too bad about Miriam. Fortunately she wasn't seriously hurt, but she had chosen the most inconvenient time to be absent from the seminary, just when she was to begin the series of lectures she had agreed to present to his advanced class. Now he would have to do the preparation himself, and gone was the opportunity to start that bit of research on the biblical origins of Western jurisprudence he had been planning. Finding time for research was a hassle. One crisis or another always seemed to interfere.

Arthur strolled along and didn't notice the large, ragged man barring his way until the two practically collided. "Pardon me," Arthur said, "I wasn't looking where I was going."

"No, no. You pardon me," the stranger said. "But first hand it all over. I mean everything, your watch, wallet, loose change, eyeglasses. Everything."

Arthur finally became aware of his surroundings. The street was busy. Pedestrians took note of the encounter and kept on walking. Drivers rolled up their car windows and stared straight ahead. Children in the street looked at them for a moment, then went on with their games. Adults chatted in doorways or looked on from windows overhead, but were unmoved by his plight, which was not so dramatic, apparently, as the soap operas being watched in nearby apartments. No one intervened. It took Arthur a moment to realize that he was being mugged but he had the good sense not to argue or resist. He emptied his pockets and, most regretfully, parted with his eyeglasses. The mugger pocketed it all and sauntered off, unhurriedly, leaving Arthur to figure out what to do next. He had no money, not even spare change. He would walk to the hospital, get to a telephone, and find someone at the seminary to drive him home—after he had visited Miriam.

Arthur started off toward the hospital, grateful he hadn't been injured, but quite upset about the mugger's insolence. After all, what use had he of Arthur's eyeglasses? That was pure malevolence. He hadn't walked far when a second man accosted him. This time Arthur knew what was coming, but it was all getting faintly absurd. What would this second fellow do when he discovered that Arthur had nothing left to donate?

"Let's have everything you've got," the second one said. This new mugger was less confident of his powers of persuasion. He revealed a knife.

"Right now, that would be nothing but the clothes on my back."

"Don't get cute with me. Just empty your pockets."

"Unfortunately," Arthur replied, "my pockets have already been emptied by that gentleman across the street."

The first mugger was leaning nonchalantly against a lamp post, watching, and smirking.

"He got to me first, shortly after I came out of the train station."

"Yeah. Well I'm going to wipe that sick smile off of his face! This is my territory."

The thwarted mugger crossed the street and waved his knife menacingly in front of the other fellow. Arthur could see they were both getting terribly aroused. He shouted to them, "Stop it, you two! Someone is going to get hurt." He thrust himself between the two, surprising them. Onlookers began to gather. This was out of the ordinary.

The second mugger pushed Arthur aside. "Get out of the way before you get hurt. I'm going to teach this son of a bitch to stay out of my territory."

The first mugger held his ground. "I saw this guy before you did and I cashed him. I never heard anyone owned this part of the street."

"Well, you heard it now."

This was a complex jurisdictional dispute of the sort Arthur specialized in. The crowd was caught up in it too, with sentiment apparently split between the two contenders.

"Wait, wait," Arthur interjected, somehow managing to stay between the two and to avoid the knife. "There's no need to kill each other. What we need to do here is to negotiate. Just listen to me."

The men, distracted, startled, stepped back. "That's better," Arthur said. He turned to the first assailant. "You have intruded into territory that, by common understanding, is the domain of this other gentleman. He has the right to feel aggrieved, mitigated by the fact that you may not have realized you were invading an area to which he had a prior claim. On the other hand, you did get to me first, and that gives you some priority."

The two muggers, now side by side in an attitude of puzzled disbelief, stared at the older man who was lecturing at them as though they were his students. He continued.

"I think I can find a way to negotiate out of this dilemma that will satisfy both of you." He turned to the first mugger. "But first I will insist that you return my eyeglasses, which have no material value to you in any event."

Someone in the crowd said, "You low life. What did you take this old man's glasses for? Give them back."

The first mugger sheepishly returned the glasses.

"That's better," said Arthur. "Now, let's get on with the negotiation. Each of you has a legitimate claim to my belongings, but violence is no solution. It rarely is, and is especially unnecessary in this situation. I propose, instead, that you simply share in the loot. I'm sure there is enough for you both."

He turned to the first mugger. "Young man, you show him what you stole from me and then divide it between you."

The two adversaries looked at each other for a moment, then at the crowd who were nodding approvingly. The second mugger relaxed his grip on the knife. "What are you," he said to Arthur, "some kind of judge?"

"No, no," Arthur replied. "I have nothing to do with the law. I'm a rabbi, and a teacher."

Arthur watched as his belongings were spilled out onto the street and the new partners negotiated their distribution. He left them to make the final arrangements and started walking up the block toward the hospital. None of the onlookers bothered him. One of them called out, "Solomon's got nothing on you, brother."

The knife-wielding mugger looked up. "Hey, where are you going, Rabbi?"

"To the hospital, to visit a colleague. That's where I was headed before I met you two gentlemen."

"Wait up," the mugger said. "You shouldn't be walking around here by yourself. This is a dangerous neighborhood. You could get hurt. We'll walk you down there."

"If it's not too much trouble," said Arthur.

The three of them set off together, the elderly Jewish scholar in the middle, under the protection of his two foot soldiers. They brought him in sight of the hospital, and then turned back, after taking leave of him.

"You take care of yourself, Rabbi."

"Yeah, take care."

What an incredible afternoon, thought Arthur. Miriam will be fascinated. I don't know what Philip will have to say, except that it will surely be disapproving.

He walked to the hospital, stopped at the information desk, and discovered that Miriam was not registered there. After a moment's confusion he prevailed on the receptionist to let him use the telephone and called back to the seminary. His secretary informed him that he had gone to the wrong hospital. He needed Eitel Hospital. Eitel Hospital, the receptionist told him, was seven or eight blocks further down, on the same street.

Not terribly far, he assured himself, as he set out walking again.

Shabbos in Brooklyn

WHENEVER BUSINESS TOOK Lillian near New York, she would extend the trip to spend a night with her Uncle Aaron and Aunt Leah, the only relatives left of her father's large family. Now Lillian was visiting her uncle and aunt after a day in the corporate offices in Connecticut. As always, they were delighted to see her.

"Let me look at you," her uncle exclaimed. "How long has it been since we saw each other?"

"Too long," her aunt interjected. "Much too long."

"Yes," Lillian agreed. "But here I am. And you both look wonderful."

"At our age, it's a wonder we can look at all," Aaron remarked. "But never mind. We are happy we get to see you again."

"And if you came with your husband," Leah added, "it would be even more wonderful."

Lillian, who was single, smiled at the familiar gibe. "If I had a husband, I would be sure to bring him along," she said.

"We'll talk about these important matters later," Aaron said, "over wine and a Shabbos dinner. But now I have to leave for shul. Maybe you want to come along, and have a look at the old synagogue?"

Years earlier Lillian's father, Jack, had been hired to paint the interior of the synagogue. "Of course," she said. "I'd love to."

The walk to the synagogue was not far, only a few blocks, but Aaron had to catch his breath and rest at each corner. Lillian noticed that Izzy's candy store was now a convenience store. The old market was gone. No kosher butcher shops or bakeries remained. Many of the apartments were already decorated for Christmas, a week before Thanksgiving.

"Everything has changed, Uncle Aaron, the neighborhood has changed."

"You should come see us more often, then you wouldn't notice so much the change. For me, the main thing is that the blocks seem to be getting longer."

When they finally arrived at the synagogue, Lillian was glad that her uncle needed a moment before attempting the steps. It gave her a chance to look at the building. She recalled the crowds who had gathered there in years past, the sea of yarmulkes and prayer shawls on the High Holy Days, the crowds of young boys and girls in their holiday best, congregating on the front steps, dashing into the street and back to the steps, their new clothes soon rumpled and askew. Now the building looked forsaken. Paint was peeling; broken windows had not been repaired. They entered from a side door. The front entrance was locked, the iron gate bolted.

The men who had come for the evening minyan assembled in a small room, formerly a classroom. Lillian remembered the large, spacious sanctuary with its polished wood, stained glass windows depicting the major Jewish holidays, and the women's balcony where she often sat squeezed between her mother and aunt, her attention half on the service and half contemplating the freedom of the front steps. Her mother, the daughter of a rabbi in the old country, let her attention stray from her prayer book only occasionally, to be sure Lillian's father hadn't sneaked out for a forbidden cigarette.

When Aaron and Lillian arrived there were a dozen elderly men already assembled. There were no other women. A single child, perhaps seven or eight years old, sat with his grandfather.

One of the men stepped to the front and began chanting the prayers in Hebrew. The others chimed in at their own pace, only occasionally glancing at the well-worn prayer books. The melodies and prayers were familiar and Lillian had little difficulty following along. She felt pleased with herself until she noticed that the youngster was also chanting the service—from memory.

Afterward her uncle introduced her around. "Harry, you remember my brother Jack. This is his daughter, Lillian, my niece."

"Nice to meet you. Sure I remember Jack, but now you mention it, I haven't seen him in a long time. Where's he been?"

One of the others piped in, "What do you mean, 'Where's he been?' He died more than two years ago."

"No," Harry said.

"What do you mean, 'No'? You were there. You were at the funeral."

"No."

"I'm telling you. Wasn't he there, Aaron?"

Aaron wasn't about to get into the middle of this. "There, not there. What does it matter? Jack is gone, that's all. Now, a good Shabbos to all."

As they walked out, Lillian commented, "I was glad to be back, but it's sad to see how run-down the synagogue is."

"You're right," Aaron said. "And the people are not doing too good either, and there are no young ones to carry on. Next time you come I'm afraid you'll see a parking lot, or a church, instead of a synagogue."

As they walked on Lillian noticed a car moving very slowly in the same direction they were going.

"Uncle Aaron, am I imagining it, or is there a car following us?"

Her uncle didn't even turn around. "You're not imagining. That's Mr. Simonetti. He owns the barber shop on the corner."

"I remember Mr. Simonetti, but why is he following us?"

"Your aunt gave him orders to follow us. Leah decided it isn't safe anymore to walk home alone at night, so she hires Mr. Simonetti to follow me when I come home from shul. It's foolish, but she said, 'No Simonetti, no Shabbos meal.' So now I have company every Friday night. At first he insisted to give me a ride. I finally convinced him that I can't ride on Shabbos."

"Maybe it's not foolish," Lillian said. "I noticed something else that bothers me. There is also a man, a very large black man, behind us. Unless Aunt Leah hired him too, I think he's also following us."

"You're as bad as your aunt. It's a street. On the street, people walk. It's near a black neighborhood, so some of the people are black."

Lillian was concerned. She had the distinct impression that the man was catching up, closing in on them. If he meant them some harm, Mr. Simonetti would be of little help. He was the same age, and about as vigorous, as Uncle Aaron.

Aaron had his mind on other matters. "Lillian, I don't like to interfere but, as Leah said, it would be nice if we had a simcha, something to look forward to—like a wedding."

"I know, Uncle Aaron, but since Morris decided he needed more time and we called off the engagement, I don't have any interest in starting to date again. My work keeps me busy."

"Well, like I said, it's not my business, but the guy who gets you would be lucky. Morris is not the only fellow in the world."

By now, Lillian was only half listening. The man who had been following them was obviously getting closer. "Uncle Aaron, that black man I mentioned is still behind us. I'm getting nervous. Maybe just this once we should let Mr. Simonetti pick us up."

"No, no. We can't ride on Shabbos."

"I don't think that fellow is just walking in the same direction. He may be after money."

"What money?" Aaron said. "I don't carry money on Shabbos."

"He doesn't know that, Uncle Aaron, and I doubt that he's *shomer Shabbos*."

The stranger was gaining on them. She knew it would be foolish to try to run. Aaron couldn't go more than a few steps and Mr. Simonetti would be of no use at all. Their pursuer had quickened his pace and she could sense that he was directly behind her. There was no escape. She felt a hand on her shoulder and turned to confront the assailant, ready to let out a piercing scream. She stared into the dark, troubled face of the black man who had been shadowing them.

Before she could utter a word, the man said, quietly, "I don't want to frighten you and the old man, but I've been watching for a couple of blocks. There's a big blue car that's been following you. I don't know if it means trouble, but if you need any help, I'll be right behind you."

Mr. Simonetti noticed that his charges were being detained. He stopped the car and tried to rush to their defense. He was trapped behind his steering wheel. By the time he extricated himself, Lillian and her uncle were shaking hands with the stranger and moving on in the direction of home.

"It's OK, Mr. Simonetti," Lillian called out. "Uncle Aaron and I are fine. We don't need any more protection. Give my regards to the family."

When they finally arrived home, Leah fussed at them. "Why are you so late? Everything is getting cold." Aaron recounted their adventure. "Mr. Simonetti got so worked up, I was afraid he would have a heart attack. In the end the black man, the one he was going to save us from, had to help him back into his car."

"You see," Leah said. "It's just as I told you. It was a good thing Mr. Simonetti was there."

"But Leah," Aaron said, "It was all a misunderstanding. The man..."

"Never mind," Leah interrupted. "Please come to the table. I already lit candles."

Aaron intoned the kiddush over a cup of wine and blessed the challah. Leah brought out the first steaming, aromatic dish, the soup with chicken that fell off the bone, and the Sabbath meal began. At the conclusion of the meal, Aaron chanted the *birkat*, the prayer of thanksgiving. Lillian joined in at the appropriate places. Uncle Aaron's voice, so like her father's, reminded her of the Friday nights in her own home when she was growing up. Even the squabbling between her aunt and uncle brought back memories that now, with the passage of time, filled her with nostalgia.

Those days were so long ago, she thought to herself, and so different from her life now: single, busy, striving, wrapped up in her career. She would not trade her current life for what seemed a simpler, more ordered existence. That was inconceivable. But nonetheless, it was pleasant and comforting to be fussed over by her aunt and uncle, steeped for this short interval in the family rituals of her youth. Yes, it was good to spend a Shabbos in Brooklyn.

A Most Fragile Friendship

MRS. LAGANO AND Mrs. Levy lived in the same four-family house in Brooklyn. At one time the house, and indeed much of the neighborhood, had been peopled by immigrant Jews from Austria, Russia, Romania, or Poland. Now the building was divided between Jews and Italians. It was hard at first for Mrs. Levy to live among gentiles, but it would have been harder still to move. She adjusted, and eventually she and Mrs. Lagano became friends. They had much in common. Each had lost a husband years before and had not remarried. Each had a child who had grown and left. Neither could fully understand how an only son could leave his mother, leave New York, and travel to some distant state. And, in a neighborhood that was again becoming filled with young mothers and bawling children, they were drawn together by their age and the recognition that they didn't quite belong. They had become the crotchety old folks who complained of the noise, the toys strewn on the steps, and the children who darted in front of cars in reckless pursuit of a stray ball.

Mrs. Lagano was a hospitable woman who enjoyed a good conversation over a cup of coffee. She visited her neighbor often, but could not prevail on her to reciprocate. On the rare occasions when Mrs. Levy called on her friend, the elderly Jewish woman would take a glass of water, but nothing more. The reason was no mystery. Mrs. Levy kept a kosher home and observed the dietary laws even outside of her own home. She had no patience for those who had one set of rules for inside and another for outside. She chastised her daughter-in-law:

"How is it that shrimp is *treyf* in the house but kosher when you eat it in a Chinese restaurant? What kind of a benediction do you make that turns treyf into kosher?"

The daughter-in-law argued: "What I do in a restaurant is one thing, and my house is another. In my house, I'm kosher."

"And what about your stomach?" asked Mrs. Levy. "Do you bring it back, full of pork and shrimp, into your 'kosher' home? Or maybe, like a cow, you've got two stomachs, one for kosher and one for treyf?"

The conflict was never resolved, except that now the daughter-in-law was a thousand miles away, doing what she pleased.

"That's the way with the younger generation," Mrs. Levy complained to her sympathetic friend. "Because they can walk on the moon, they think they can make miracles. But kosher from treyf, they can't make."

Though it became increasingly difficult, Mrs. Levy kept to her ways. She now had to walk blocks to the Jewish butcher. Once there had been a bakery on almost every corner. Now she had to take a bus to get a challah for Friday night. Before Passover, she risked her neck on a rickety stool as she replaced the ordinary dishes with the Passover service.

Mrs. Lagano watched with alarm. "Edna," she said. "You'll hurt yourself. You're too old to be climbing up and down with boxes."

Mrs. Levy had no time for arguments. "Please, Mrs. Lagano, I have work to do. It's almost Passover already, and nothing is ready. When I can no longer make Passover, I hope I'll be gone from this earth."

Mrs. Lagano offered no further protests. Mrs. Levy was right. You don't stop living when you get old. You don't give up the things you have done all your life, or else it's no life at all. Her own children had urged her to bring in a housekeeper—a stranger to do her work! They wanted to make an invalid out of her. If she couldn't clean, cook, turn a piece of cloth into a garment, how could she stay alive? Like Mrs. Levy, she knew that when she could no longer care for herself and her home, it would be all over.

Of course, the two friends had their disagreements. Each had too long been the sole proprietor of her own life to bend easily. Mrs. Levy liked to shop on Eighteenth Avenue, Mrs. Lagano on Eighty-Sixth Street. Mrs. Lagano liked to sit out on a bench in front of the stoop on warm nights; Mrs. Levy preferred the comfort of her air-conditioned bedroom. Still, they were inseparable. They had known the desolation of having words to say but no ears to receive them, of haunting the mailbox for a letter or a card from a son, of hoping for a chance encounter with an acquaintance. Together, they formed a barrier against the loneliness that was so ready to envelop them.

One was a pious Jew, the other a devout Catholic. Years earlier, it would have been unthinkable that they should become friends, or even get to know each other. Now, differences in background and religion seemed insignificant in face of the solace they provided each other. Their religious differences were recognized but scarcely mentioned. There was no need. Each practiced in her own ways without intruding on the other, without the need to explain or to justify. Let the philosophers have arguments about religion. For such friends as Mrs. Levy and Mrs. Lagano, discourses on religion were superfluous—until Mrs. Levy's ancient stove, her faithful servant, expired.

Mrs. Levy took the demise of her stove badly. A good friend had been lost; a constant companion for more than three decades. That stove had seen her son grow from childhood into maturity. It had been the instrument of her most precious moments—triumphs in cooking and baking that she still could recreate in her mind. How many dozens of cookies had she baked for bar mitzvahs and weddings? How many bowls of chicken soup had flowed from that stove? And now it was gone, kaput, a part of the past.

She brought the sad news to Mrs. Lagano, who was considerably less romantic.

"Edna! Why are you carrying on over a piece of tin with heartburn in the middle? You'll get a new stove. Why the fuss?"

"You don't understand," Mrs. Levy said. "That stove was part of my family; it's older than my Lenny. What do I want with these new contraptions with all the dials and buttons. I'm too old to learn to cook all over again."

"So that's it!" Mrs. Lagano exclaimed. "You're worried you won't have your touch with a new stove. You're afraid it will be too complicated for you. Admit it."

Mrs. Levy pouted. "I just don't want a fancy new stove at this time of my life."

"Edna, there's no need to be nervous about a new stove. You'll catch on right away. You'll be a better cook even than before. A regular gourmet."

Mrs. Levy allowed herself to be comforted. After all, it would be something to look forward to, a new stove after so long. Who knows what triumphs she might create? She could already savor the delight of turning out the first batch of cookies she would send to Lenny. Her face lit with a smile of anticipation.

Mrs. Lagano, delighted that she had been able to reassure her friend, pressed on.

"I know you'll be a great success. Meanwhile, until you get your new one, you can cook on my stove."

There was a sudden silence as Mrs. Levy looked at her friend. Then, with great effort, she said, "You know I can't cook on your stove."

"Of course you can. Mine is the same as your old one. You'll be right at home."

Mrs. Levy was confused. Could it be that her friend truly didn't understand? "Please," Mrs. Levy said, "I can't use your stove. You know I can't."

Mrs. Lagano was hurt. "What's wrong with my stove? It doesn't have a disease. It's clean. I take care the same as you. In all the years we've known each other, you have never once taken a bite in my house. It's like I'm infected with something."

"Olga! Please don't go on. I don't want to argue. I don't want to insult you. I just can't cook on your stove. It's not that it's dirty or any such thing. It's just that it's not kosher. So I can't do it. It's nothing to do with you."

Mrs. Lagano didn't respond.

Mrs. Levy started for the door. "Well, Mrs. Lagano, I'll be leaving now. Soon it will be dark, and time for me to light the candles. It gets dark so early...About the stove, thank you for the offer. But, you see, I can't accept. I don't mean to hurt you, and it's not personal, but, for me, your stove—well, I can't use it."

Her voice broke. She fled the apartment without looking at her friend, who made no effort to stop her.

In due time Mrs. Levy acquired her new stove; and in due time she mastered its intricacies. Mrs. Lagano had been right. She carefully packed the first batch of cookies in a sturdy, crush-proof box, and mailed them to Lenny with a prayer they would be whole and fresh when they arrived.

The next batch she arranged on a paper plate, with tinfoil over them. She had not spoken with Mrs. Lagano these several weeks. The two women had even managed to avoid meeting each other, a remarkable feat considering their proximity and how long they had synchronized the rhythm of their lives. Mrs. Levy learned from one of the other tenants that Mrs. Lagano had been sick. A bad cold. And there had been some problem with Mrs. Lagano's grandchild in California, but the neighbor was uncertain of the details. Neither had made any effort at reconciliation though they both felt a loneliness even greater than before they had become friends.

"What can I say to her?" Mrs. Levy asked herself. "Should I try to explain the dietary laws? Should I tell her again it was nothing personal? Some things have to be accepted as they are, not defended or explained. But should a stove stand between two old friends, 'a piece of tin with heartburn in the middle'?" She smiled when she remembered Mrs. Lagano's remark.

All of these thoughts crossed Mrs. Levy's mind as she approached Mrs. Lagano's apartment and carefully placed the plate of cookies at the doorstep, gently so as not to disturb the arrangement, as though the plate contained something precious and irreplaceable—as precious and irreplaceable as a friendship. Mrs. Levy hesitated a moment. "I hope she likes them. They are good cookies, even if I say so myself." Then she rang the bell and retreated to her own apartment. She quickly closed her door and was hidden from view. She could not see the expression on Mrs. Lagano's face when she found the offering at her doorstep.

It was a quiet afternoon. There were no sounds from the street, no cars passing by; the children were still in school. She waited expectantly, impatiently for a knock or a ring.

Sign of the Covenant

IN THE ANTISEPTIC corridors of the maternity ward at University Hospital something new, and yet infinitely old, was about to take place. Joseph Pauker, fourth-born and the only male child to Jerry and Roz Pauker, was about to be circumcised in the traditional manner, by a mohel rather than a medical doctor, and the bris was to take place in the hospital. For the first time, a non-physician was allowed to use the hospital facilities for a surgical procedure. Doctors, nurses, and ward clerks mixed with relatives and friends of the family to view the enactment of this timeless rite in a modern medical facility. It was a mixed assembly, old and young, Jews and gentiles, medical professionals and lay persons.

For the family, it was an occasion for joy, marking the entry of their son into the covenant first prescribed for Father Abraham. There was another emotion as well, born of the knowledge that it is through a wound inflicted on the body that the child makes his entry into the covenant. Though it may last only a moment, the pain is there, standing guard at the passageway.

A section of the maternity ward had been set aside and transformed into a banquet space. Surgical tables were covered with white cloths and bedecked with flowers and all manner of foods: cakes, cookies, candies, breads, cheese, and even whiskey and wine. Visitors milled around, uncertain whether to partake of the food before the ceremony, awaiting the mohel and the start of the procedure.

The mohel arrived in a bustle of activity. He immediately plunged into the assembled throng, taking its measure as an actor measures the audience in a theater. This was indeed his proscenium, and he relished it. He was in his late fifties, well above six feet tall, with a dark,

215

ruddy face, a slight mustache, and a striking presence. For decades he had been performing circumcisions in the Jewish community, and along with his surgical skills he had developed a style that had more than a trace of the theatric. He quickly took charge, keenly aware that he was being observed by members of the medical profession, including several foreign doctors who were visiting American hospitals. This was a stage worthy of his talents and his voice swelled to match his enthusiasm.

"Once I wanted to be a surgeon," he confided in his booming voice. "But how can a poor immigrant family afford to send a son to medical school? So, you see, I became a surgeon anyway. Not only a surgeon, but a specialist."

He smiled, enjoying his own joke.

"And let me tell you, I know my business. I've performed this operation thousands of times, all over the Midwest. Doctors come to me to learn how I do it. Christians too. Not only Jews."

He admonished one of the nurses. "No, the baby will be here, where the light is better, not over there. And the sterilized instruments here. Good. Good. And you, nurse, you stand by in case I need you. Not for the baby, but sometimes someone in the crowd gets a little light in the head."

He turned to the child's father. "Who is to be sandek? Who will hold the baby?"

A man in his late thirties stepped forward, his face a bit ashen, matching the color of his hair. The mohel pantomimed the proper grip.

"You'll hold the child so…" He looked at the sandek disapprovingly. "I don't want any problems from you. No fainting. I need to concentrate on the baby." The sandek-designate blanched at the suggestion.

All was ready. The audience was properly dispersed. The threat of calamity had been raised. The professionals were given places at the mohel's side. He surveyed the scene, looking for likely weaklings, allowing his gaze to linger particularly on those he recognized as gentile, instructing them with his gaze: Take note. This is the way we do it. This is the way it must be done.

It was time. The infant was brought in. The crowd froze and then sighed at the sight of the baby, just eight days old, his eyes squinting in the light, cradled in the arms of his grandfather. The child was placed on a board across the sandek's knees. His blanket and diaper were removed.

The mohel held his hands delicately in the air as the nurse placed surgical gloves on his long fingers. His hands lingered dramatically in this position even after the gloves were on.

"First," the mohel announced, "we give little Joseph something to make him calm." He instructed the nurse to place a gauze, dipped in sweet, kosher wine, into a nipple, and then to hand the nipple to the child's mother.

"When I tell you, you'll just put the nipple to his lips, and he'll be fine. And don't worry, we won't make a *shikker* out of him." He smiled at the titter than ran through the assembly. He turned to one of the doctors. "You see, we know about anesthetic, too."

He peered at the sandek who now had hold of the infant's feet. "Good. Just like that." Then he turned to the crowd.

"All right, we'll begin. But please, step back a little so that the doctors can see. It's very important that they should be able to see without obstruction."

There was a moment's hubbub as several persons changed places, those in front seeking the more serene comfort of the rear; those behind now suddenly finding themselves pressed into closer proximity than they desired.

After asking the father if he had permission to perform the bris in the father's stead, as required by the tradition, he chanted a blessing in Hebrew and signaled the nurse to lower his surgical mask. He reached for a scalpel, looked up once more at the assembly, and bent toward his task…but suddenly he was arrested by a dull thump. One of the men in the rear had crumpled. Fortunately, his neighbor had intercepted his fall and laid him gently on the floor. In an instant the nurse attended to him and, sheepish, the man was helped out of the room, more embarrassed than injured.

The mohel was unperturbed. As soon as the man was gone he worked rapidly and deftly, talking all the while, extolling the qualities of the instruments he was using, tracing their evolution during his long career, drawing attention to the particulars of his technique, gesticulating for the doctors.

The infant let out one cry of protest but was immediately quieted by the nipple. How long did it take? Minutes perhaps, but minutes of uncertain duration so that time could not be fairly measured, at once endless and no more than a deep, grateful breath. When it was done, past and present melded, and the corridor became a sanctuary. Then, suddenly, there was movement, breath exhaled, noise, shouts of "Mazel tov! Mazel tov!" Anxious faces lit with smiles. The room was again a blur of sounds and activity as people reached out to congratulate the parents.

Among the Jews it was affirmed that, with God's help, they would assemble again for Joseph's bar mitzvah and when he stood under the marriage canopy. After a slight hesitation the guests converged on the festive tables. The wine flowed. The guests clapped each other on the shoulder, calling each other's name, as though in it were some kind of blessing. Some became a bit tipsy and laughter could be heard up and down the halls. Even the sandek was congratulated as though he too had performed a delicate operation.

His work done, the mohel retreated to a corner of the corridor, no longer the center of attention. The sandek, fortified by a sip of whiskey, discovered him and praised his skill.

"Yes," he acknowledged, "it takes skill. And work, too. Hard work and study. It's not just a gift. It takes learning and practice."

He lowered his voice to a hushed whisper. "You know that man who fainted? For a minute I thought to myself—he's in the right position…" He again smiled at his own joke, and then gathered his instruments and prepared to leave.

The sandek slipped quietly away to extend one last mazel tov to the parents and to gaze into the face of Joseph. The child slept quietly, but for an instant his eyes fluttered open and the sandek imagined he could see the trace of a smile.

"Welcome," the sandek said softly. "Welcome, and have a long and good life."

Going Kosher

SOON AFTER SHE came to America, my maternal grandmother announced that "kosher means clean" and thereafter she dedicated her religious fervor to a holy war against *shmutz* of every kind. By her own definition she was a religious fanatic, but that didn't translate into a separation between meat and dairy dishes. My mother's attitude was similar. I don't mean to suggest that we had no restrictions. Some foods we never ate: pork, because pigs wallow in mud; shellfish because civilized people don't eat insects; crawly things because—because they're crawly things. We didn't have meat and dairy on the same table, but no one counted the hours, or the minutes between them.

Eileen, on the other hand, came from a home in which the dietary laws were scrupulously observed. Her mother had four bowls for the mixer: meat and dairy and another set for Passover. She also had four sets of dishtowels, different soap dishes, different scouring pads, and so on. My father-in-law was a self-employed painter who was frequently between jobs, but never idle. My mother-in-law kept him busy changing cabinets, moving walls, adding shelves, in the perpetual attempt to find more room or a better arrangement for the dishes.

The first year we were married, Eileen and I lived in Brooklyn, close to both sets of parents. Despite Eileen's earlier experiences, our kitchen wasn't kosher. When my in-laws came to visit, they always brought their own food, "leftovers," they would insist. We gave them the greatest pleasure, however, when we ate at their house, so that they could be sure not only that we ate the proper foods, but also in the proper quantities, which meant until we ached. Then the tea was served, with a piece of cake, of course. How could one drink dry tea?

We were married a year when we moved to Iowa City, Iowa, so that I could continue my graduate studies in speech pathology. We lived on the scant income I received as a research assistant and Eileen could earn at odd jobs. Kashruth was scarcely on our minds as we scraped for every penny. We received packages from home and wept when the kosher pastrami came out of the tinfoil wrapping covered with green mold, and we scraped away the mold to see what we could rescue beneath it.

During our second year at the university we were hired as caretakers of Hillel. Each Sunday evening we oversaw a communal meal for the students, but even at Hillel at that time there was little attention to keeping kosher. Early in the year a young Jewish student from New York arrived with two suitcases, one filled with clothes, the other with dried kosher salami to tide him over while he searched for an Orthodox family with whom to board. Alas, he never found a host and by the year's end he was attended by the powerful aroma of garlic.

It was through our children that we finally considered going kosher. When they were quite young we moved to Minneapolis. At first, the pots and pans we carried across the country, given as a wedding gift by Uncle Meyer and Aunt Ann, cooked meat and dairy indifferently and we were no closer to keeping kosher than before. The turning point came when we joined Adath Jeshurun Synagogue, enrolled our children in Talmud Torah, and became increasingly involved in synagogue life. Even then, we changed slowly. One doesn't embrace kashruth after so many years of neglect without discussion, arguments, deliberation:

It doesn't make sense—It makes spiritual sense.

It's an anachronism—It's an affirmation.

It sets us apart—It binds us together.

We don't have space—We can make space.

It's a lot of effort—Advantage comes from effort.

It's expensive—It's expensive.

The turning didn't become a full turn until after David's bar mitzvah. After, not before. David is our firstborn and the first grandchild on either side of the family. The New York relatives came to Minnesota for the occasion and were properly impressed with David's skill in conducting the service, reading Torah and Haftorah, and his ease in front of the congregation. That evening we had a catered dinner at our house for the out-of-town guests. Alongside the catered dinner, my mother-in-law had brought her own chopped liver, a sumptuous brisket, and various other of her specialties, and she engaged in a brisk trade among the guests, to the chagrin of the non-Jewish caterer who had made an effort to prepare Jewish-style dishes. Eileen's mother was irrepressible:

"Before you eat that, try this. Good, no? You can't beat kosher chopped liver. How about a piece of brisket: No, no, not that. Real brisket. From New York. The knishes? Of course I made them myself…"

It dawned on us that something was wrong. At least one set of parents and some of our children's friends would not eat the food we prepared. The rabbi couldn't eat in our home. It isn't right, we finally understood, to have a home in which all of our Jewish friends wouldn't feel comfortable. We had worked hard at convincing our children that a bar mitzvah is a religious celebration, not simply a large party with guests and gifts. At the same time we were lecturing them, we were giving the children the wrong message. We decided to go kosher.

The process of converting to a kosher home enriched the neighborhood. The chicken noodle soup went to one neighbor, the canned ravioli to another, the cake and pie mixes with suspect ingredients to still another. We also enriched local stores. Silver and dishes that we could not buy new were boiled and then sorted according to principles that would have challenged a cognitive scientist, based on color and the location of chips and other imperfections. We were given Passover dishes by Eileen's mother, who was delighted, and our kitchen was never cleaner. Just when I was adjusting to my first bifocals I had to strain to read the labels on cans and wrappings of bakery products.

Meanwhile, the word went out to the synagogue community as though carried by fiery messengers. We were acclaimed and congratulated by some, and greeted with incredulity by others, Jews and non-Jews, who didn't know what to make of this transformation.

"You mean we can't store our meat in your freezer?"

"We can't have a potluck at your home unless it's all dairy? And fish is OK with dairy but not chicken? Are you sure you have that right?"

"What do you mean no crab? Isn't crab a fish?"

"How can you do this to our gourmet club?"

"And this religion has lasted four thousand years?"

In the process of going kosher the kitchen had to be remodeled. My deceased father-in-law would have loved that job and would have appreciated the work done by "Ole" Swanson, an old-fashioned craftsman. Because mine is the more compulsive nature, and despite the difference in our backgrounds, I became the most fastidious and intrusively vigilant, peering over Eileen's shoulder at the grocery store, checking and rechecking the position of chips on the dishes and geometric patterns on the silverware. Eileen settled into a pattern of repining observance, marked by occasional outbursts that it is all impossible and impoverishing and to be endured only until the children are grown and out of the house.

A little more than a year after David's bar mitzvah, we had a bat mitzvah for Karen, and five years after that, a bar mitzvah for Josh. We now had a kosher home, but my mother-in-law brought her own chopped liver anyway, because there is still a difference between kosher and delicious. We still haven't gotten around to inviting the new rabbi and his lovely family for dinner. The children no longer live at home—two are married with children of their own. Keeping kosher is expensive. Kosher meat is very costly and there are fewer kosher butchers in Minneapolis than before. Perhaps we were all intended to be vegetarians after all. The gourmet club did succumb, though I don't think our dietary habits were the entire reason. We were all getting too old to be gourmets. I now read labels through trifocals, but still we persevere. I have discovered what I knew all along. I keep kosher not for the children, but for myself.

In Search of a
Friday-Night Challah

"TELL ME WHAT you eat, and I'll tell you what you are," said the French gastronome Anthelme Brillat-Savarin. True enough, but for Jews that's not the end of the story. We Jews are defined as much by the foods we don't eat as by those we do. We are commanded that we may eat the flesh of only certain animals, and even then only if they were unblemished and were slaughtered in a certain way, and even then only certain parts of the animal, and even then only if the meat is not served with certain other foods. Even I, who grew up in a non-kosher home, learned the cultural taboos: lobsters and spiders have an overwhelming family resemblance. Snails and oysters are other-world creatures of darkness. Squirrels and rabbits share a condominium with mice and rats. I could no more eat one than the others. To quote my sage grandmother, who could speak paragraphs in a single word, "Phehhh!"

Sometimes I am at a committee meeting away from home and at the day's end the chairman says, in an effusion of goodwill, "Let's all go out together to celebrate our accomplishments. I know a wonderful, authentic Chinese restaurant that tourists rarely go to."

In the spirit of camaraderie, I go along, knowing too well how stingily I will dine. In the restaurant, the chairman reveals himself as an expert on authentic Chinese cooking and a good friend of the chef. He joyfully insists that he will order for all of us. The parade of dishes begins and I pass up the fried rice, egg rolls, breaded shrimp, lobster claws, sweet and sour pork, and other delicacies, eating plain white rice and drinking green tea while my colleagues enthusiastically wield forks, fingers, and chopsticks.

"Are you sure you won't try any of this?" the chairman says solicitously. "There's very little pork in it."

My aversion to certain foods is not solely because they are listed among the unclean animals in Deuteronomy. My tastes were shaped by my aforementioned grandmother who was an authority on cleanliness. Her influence was indelible. Once she pronounced a certain food unclean, no logic or further experience could change that judgment for me, strive as I might to become more universal or sophisticated. Pigs, my grandmother assured me, are filthy animals. Never mind that chickens are filthier than pigs. It is a great mystery of Jewish life that the chicken from which chicken soup is made purifies itself as well as everything else with which it comes into contact. Nothing can redeem a pig, but a kosher chicken, when added to a pot of water and just enough onion, garlic and fresh soup greens (not too much celery), is transformed.

In my youth, in one of those small but momentous experiences that pushes the boy toward the man, when values are in stark opposition and there is no escaping the need to choose, I once ate a pork chop. My high-school speech teacher had invited me to his home on Long Island. It was a great honor. I had never been to a teacher's home before. We chatted comfortably before dinner and I felt wonderfully grown up. Then we sat down to table and there in front of me was a pork chop. I had never been in such intimate relationship with a pork chop. I was reminded immediately of Stephen's Meat Market near my home. In the windows of Stephen's Meat Market were three steel barbs, like gigantic fishing hooks. On certain days of the week Stephen hung the decapitated heads of pigs from those hooks. No body, no frame, just the impaled heads facing the street, with the eyes, modestly closed.

At my teacher's table I felt as though I were face to face, snout to snout, with those impaled heads. Despite my discomfort, I talked amiably with my hosts. He was my revered teacher and I could not embarrass him. I chewed. I swallowed. But all the time I imagined those eyes staring at me from under closed lids, as though I were back at Stephen's shop. Miraculously, I succeeded. God gave me the strength to eat pork chops.

It was not until I became an adult, living far from New York and my early roots, that I began to reconcile the wisdom of Deuteronomy, the tradition, and my grandmother, with the wisdom of Anthelme Brillat-Savarin, and to look more closely at the implications of those ancient admonishments, to see how far they reached into all phases of my life: You are what you eat and what you refrain from eating; what you do, and what you will not do; what you value, and what you abhor; what you deny, and what you affirm.

It is out of this budding understanding that while I was in Santa Barbara, California, thousands of miles from Stephen's Meat Market in New York, and years distant from that evening with my speech teacher, I yearned for a Friday-night challah. Santa Barbara is a beautiful coastal city, with mountains on one side and the Pacific Ocean on the other. It is warm in the winter and cool in the summer. President Reagan had his ranch in the foothills. He retired there to ride horses, chop wood, and nap. I was there with my wife on sabbatical. We arrived in Santa Barbara on a Wednesday, and on Friday evening we went to our first Shabbat services, and missed very few during the next ten months. It was a pleasure to find and be welcomed immediately by the Jewish community. The head of the temple nursery school discovered that my wife was an experienced nursery-school teacher who had worked in Jewish schools, and soon pressed her into service. On Saturday mornings a group of mostly octogenarians conducted a more traditional worship service without the benefit of clergy, and I became part of the Shabbos morning minyan.

We found a home in the Jewish community but there was one need the community couldn't seem to meet. There was not a Jewish bakery anywhere. A Friday-night meal with candles and wine is incomplete without a challah to make the *motzi*. We tried whole-wheat bread, French bread, English muffins, sourdough bread, but none could substitute for a Jewish challah crowning the table. We briefly considered making our own. I thought it was a good project for my wife, and she for me, and so two good thoughts canceled each other and we remained with English muffins, sourdough bread, whole wheat. I yearned for a Friday-night challah.

I unburdened myself to one of the old-timers in the Shabbos morning minyan, hoping that he would be so struck with the pathos of my situation that he would volunteer his wife to bake an extra challah every week. She hadn't baked bread in ten years, he told me. They bought their challah from Lasch's bakery, the same place the temple bought it. Lasch, and his father before him, operated an old-world bakery that specialized in European breads and pastries, and didn't use forbidden lard or animal shortening. The very next Friday I bought a lovely, tasty, golden challah from Lasch's and from then on I was a regular customer. On Rosh Hashanah he baked special round challah, with raisins. Life was good.

Life was good, that is, until I became too inquisitive. My downfall was brought on by one of Lasch's rolls, a crisp, hard roll that fought back when it was bit into. I loved it and one week I asked the saleslady how it was made.

"Just flour and water and yeast," she said, "with vegetable shortening and powdered milk." She spoke with obvious pride at the quality of their products.

"I didn't know that bread is made with milk," I said.

"Oh, yes. Mr. Lasch makes all of his breads with milk."

What I had just heard seemed scarcely possible. All of the breads made with milk? Including the challah? A challah transcends ordinary bread. The rules for challah can't be the same as those for other breads. No one could bake so tempting a challah and then make it inaccessible by including milk in the recipe. Surely the rabbi or someone in the community who weekly dined on Mr. Lasch's delicious challah would have told him that observant Jews are forbidden from eating meat and dairy at the same time.

"You don't mean all of the breads," I said coaxingly. "You can't mean the challah. No one makes challah with milk."

"Yes," she said, a little annoyed with me now. "All of them."

I didn't want to believe it. That lovely challah that had given me such Sabbath pleasure could never again grace my Shabbos table. It was too cruel. Out of an innocent question about a dinner roll had come this terrible revelation.

Out of despair grew hope. Maybe, I thought, if I explained the problem to Mr. Lasch, he could modify the recipe. If I could only talk to him he would surely change the ingredients out of respect for his longtime Jewish customers. I tried vainly to call him several times, but he was always busy in the bakery. The following week I drove to the store and luckily caught him during a break in his baking.

"Mr. Lasch, my name is Siegel. I've been trying to contact you but I can never reach you by telephone, so I decided to see you in person."

"What's on your mind, Siegel?"

"Well, I'm not from here. I'm from Minnesota, but I'm living in Santa Barbara for the year. A couple of months ago I discovered your wonderful challahs and I've been buying them every week to celebrate the Jewish Sabbath."

"I'm glad you like my bread," he said. "So what's the problem?"

"I just found out something about your challah. Even though it's beautiful and delicious, I can't use it any more the way you bake it."

None of this made any sense to him. "Why not? If it's good, it's good."

I tried to explain. "Because you put milk in the dough, and Jews who follow the dietary laws—you know, who keep kosher?—they can't mix meat with milk at the same meal. I can't put your bread on the same table with any kind of meat, and on Friday nights we usually have chicken. That's also tradition, so I can't have it with your challah."

He puffed on his cigarette. "All this is news to me. That's the way I've always baked it. No one has ever complained. I even got the recipe from a Jewish fellow."

"Mr. Lasch, I don't think anyone thought to ask whether there is milk in the challah. It's so unusual. I found out by accident. Wouldn't it be possible to make the bread without milk? You would be doing a great service (I almost said mitzvah) to many people. A lot of the people who buy your challah have no idea it has milk."

I could tell he was moved and ready to consider my request. I was petitioning for a whole community, not for myself, and even though it didn't make any logical sense to him, he could acknowledge that it was for a righteous purpose. He understood the pull of tradition.

While we were talking, another shopkeeper walked by. Mr. Lasch called him over.

"Hey, Lenny, come here. Siegel here has been telling me about meat and milk and it adds up to he can't eat my bread unless I change the recipe. What do you know about it?"

Mr. Lenny Lerner, proprietor of a clothing store next to the bakery, scratched his head and looked very perplexed. Then he brightened.

"Wait," he said. "I do remember something about meat and dairy, from my grandparents. It used to be Jews couldn't mix them, but I don't think it still applies. I haven't heard about it in a long time."

That was enough for Mr. Lasch. He now had heard from his own religious authority, Mr. Lerner. The case was closed. A Jew had given him the recipe and another Jew had proclaimed it kosher.

I made one more attempt. If I could offer Mr. Lasch a commercial recipe that didn't use milk, perhaps he would try it. I knew I would need a recipe that deals in sacks, not cups of flour. I called Debbie Wolk, a kosher caterer in Minneapolis. She didn't have a recipe, but she knew who might. Gene LeVee, who used to live in Minneapolis, had recently opened a kosher bakery in Oakland, California. Gene had eaten at our home, participated in our seders, and even lived in our house for several months while we were in Israel. Professional bakers are reluctant to share their secrets, but Gene rose above such concerns. This was a community emergency. The recipe came in the mail several days later.

I now knew Mr. Lasch's routine and I caught him during his cigarette break. He wasn't happy to see me.

"Mr. Lasch," I said, "I have here a recipe for challah from a top-notch baker who bakes hundreds of loaves every week, each one a perfect gem. And it requires no milk. Not a drop. Here, look at this and see if your mouth doesn't water just reading it."

Grudgingly, Mr. Lasch looked at the recipe. For an instant I noticed a flicker of interest. But then he grunted, and pushed it back to me.

"I don't need this. I've been baking bread here for years. Everyone knows my products and nobody has ever complained. I don't need to change."

"But Mr. Lasch, won't you even…"

He put out his cigarette and turned back to his bakery without letting me finish. I never stepped into the bakery again.

WHEN I RETURNED to Minneapolis, my son questioned me about religious life in Santa Barbara.

"It was fine," I told him. "There is an active Reform congregation, and a few smaller splinter groups. Even an Orthodox congregation that prays in the rabbi's garage."

"What about the services? What were they like?"

"The melodies were different and there wasn't as much participation as we have here at home. I'm afraid I sang louder than most others, but no one objected. I was invited to join the choir they will be setting up next year. Our biggest problem was finding a challah for Friday nights."

"Why, no bakeries there?"

"Plenty of bakeries, but none that knows how to make a kosher challah."

"What did you do?"

"That's a long story. Did you ever read Ibsen's *Enemy of the People*?"

"That's a play about some guy who tries to warn a community that the water supply is poisoned or something but no one wants to hear about it. Isn't that it?"

"Well, that was me, but with a Friday-night challah. I accidentally learned that the only challah baker in town used milk in the recipe and I never could figure out what to do about it. I didn't know whether to broadcast the information, or keep it to myself."

"So what did you do?"

"Left Santa Barbara as I found it. I knew the truth, but it didn't make me free. I'm still pondering whether I ought to have made a campaign of it."

My son didn't hesitate at all. "I tell you, Pop, I'm glad you didn't. It's a nice place and I might want to visit it without changing my name or disguising my face. It's their town. They can handle it."

They can handle it. Why hadn't that occurred to me? Youth has its own wisdom. That is always such a wonderful discovery, especially in one's own children. Of course they can handle it.

If I Were a Levi

AN OLD JOKE: A man approaches the rabbi of his synagogue and says, "Rabbi, I want you to make me a *Kohane.*

"Arnold, I can't make you a Kohane. That's not up to me."

"But Rabbi, I'm willing to pay for it. I'll make a substantial donation to the synagogue."

"Arnold, I appreciate your offer, but it's out of the question. This is not something a rabbi can do."

"Maybe I didn't make myself clear. When I said a substantial contribution, I meant ten thousand dollars. Think what you can do for the congregation with that amount of money."

"Arnold, I don't know how many ways to tell you. It's not a matter of money. It's not in my power to make someone a Kohane. Either you are a Kohane or you're not."

"Rabbi, I won't beat around the bush. I'm not talking thousands now. I'm talking enough money to build the extension to the education building we've wanted for so long."

"Arnold, are you serious? That would be more than a million dollars!"

"I'm serious, Rabbi. I want to leave something when I'm gone, and this would be just the thing."

The rabbi thought for a while. A new education wing would invigorate the congregation, and it wouldn't hurt his own tenure. There had been grumbling that he no longer had the enthusiasm and energy the congregation needed, and he was still several years away from retirement. In these modern times, what did it matter, Kohane or Israelite? If the man wanted it that badly, was willing to give so much for the privilege, what would it hurt to call him a Kohane? In fact, it would be a mitzvah.

"Arnold, this is a very serious matter," the rabbi said. "But I think, under the circumstances, if you are willing to undertake the obligations of a Kohane, it could be arranged."

"Thank you, Rabbi, thank you!"

The following morning Arnold appeared in the rabbi's office and delivered a check for slightly more than a million dollars. The rabbi could hardly believe his eyes. He had never touched so much money at one time. He thanked Arnold for his generosity.

"There is just one thing, Arnold. Why are you so anxious to be a Kohane?"

"It's a family thing, Rabbi. My father was a Kohane, and his father before him, and I want to follow in their footsteps."

I NEVER ASPIRED to be a Kohane. But a Levi would have been nice. My name is Siegel, and a name that ends with "el" often signifies the tribe of Levi. But not always. Some Siegels are descended from plain old Israelites. That's the case in my family. My father was an Israelite and his father before him, so I too am an Israelite.

But not my son Josh. One summer, Josh came back from Herzl Camp and announced that with the name Siegel he was entitled to be a Levi. I told Josh that he came from a long line of Israelites and that there was even suspicion our family name had been changed at Ellis Island. It didn't matter. Josh had made up his mind. He would be a Levi.

It occurred to me that maybe I should dig deeper into my family history. I certainly didn't have any documents proving that I'm an Israelite. It's just something I always knew. The genealogy books say the first thing in figuring out a family history is to contact relatives. My father died years ago and my mother had no interest in my father's relatives because they were "kooks" (and she was not referring to the famous rabbinic family). I branched out on my own. I sent Cousin Harriet the wedding present I meant to give her seven years ago, and asked what she knew about our family history. I contacted Aunt Fanny who had been ostracized when she eloped with Mike, the milkman. I even contacted Uncle Aaron who had not been heard from since he took up ballroom dancing and married his non-Jewish partner. No one had information suggesting we belong to the tribe of Levi.

Still, my efforts weren't wasted. Uncle Aaron discovered that Aunt Fanny also loves ballroom dancing and, since she had left Mike the Milkman, and Uncle Aaron's wife had taken up with a much younger tango instructor, Aunt Fanny was willing to be his dance partner. Harriet returned the wedding present because she had already been divorced for six years and didn't need a Jell-O mold. And several of the younger members thought it would be a good idea to start up the "cousins club" again.

There is more. My wife's father was a Levi, so that makes her one. Perhaps someday it will be decided that living with a Levi for many decades is enough to make me one, too. After all, what did the Levis do? They served in the Temple and that's exactly what I've been doing for my wife all these years.

I've decided not to pursue it. I'm satisfied with my place among the Jewish people. For me, it's enough that I am a Jew. Still, I'm proud that my son is a Levi. After all, what father isn't happy to be surpassed by his own children?

This Isn't Netflix

JUST A LITTLE WHILE ago my wife and I went to the Edina Theater with our friends Susan and Tom Kafka to see the film *Tell No One*. We were a little early, and while we were waiting for the coming attractions I mentioned to Susan that I was reading *People of the Book*, a recent novel by Geraldine Brooks.

"Do you like it?" she asked.

"It's a really good book," I answered.

A woman sitting in the row in front of us turned around and said, "Are you reading *People of the Book*?"

"Yes," I answered.

"I've read it. It's a really good book," she said.

A fellow sitting behind me leaned forward and asked, "What book are you talking about?"

"*People of the Book*, by Geraldine Brooks," I answered.

"I've heard that's a really good book," he said.

"Yes," I said. And the woman behind me concurred.

I turned to my wife, who had been silently enjoying the exchange, and muttered, "They must be Jewish. Only *Yidn* would have the chutzpa to *mish arayn* (mix in) in a conversation like this."

The fellow behind me leaned forward and said, "That was Yiddish you were speaking, right? Tell me, is there a written literature in Yiddish?"

"Sure there is," I answered. "Of course."

"Tell that to my friend over there." He pointed to someone sitting across the aisle. "He says there is no Jewish literature."

"Well, there is. There's a great literary tradition in Yiddish."

The guy across the aisle took exception. "Nah. They use Hebrew characters, but there is no real language."

I was becoming indignant. "Of course it's a language. And our great writers wrote in it: Mendele, Sholom Aleichem, Peretz, Asch. Even Isaac Bashevis Singer wrote his books and stories in Yiddish and then had them translated."

"Are you a professor?" the guy behind me asked.

"I was. At the University of Minnesota. I'm retired."

He turned triumphantly to his friend. "He's a professor, and he says there is a Yiddish literature."

The fellow across the aisle was not impressed. "No way," he said.

I was going to join the argument again, even more forcefully, but then the movie began. At first I had a little trouble concentrating. I was thinking about our conversation. How strange to find myself among people I didn't know and to be speaking, arguing, about Yiddish. When the movie ended, the fellow behind me said, "It was nice talking with you." He and his wife and the couple across the aisle left. I don't know which I enjoyed more, the movie or the encounter with these strangers.

It's good to leave the Netflix behind and step out to a theater sometimes, no? To be with old friends and watch the movie, and then have a good cup of tea and a good conversation about it afterward: What did this mean? What did that mean? Why did that character do that at just that time? Really? I hadn't noticed that! Now it makes sense, but then why did she...?

And it's also nice to speak a little Yiddish while you're there because who can tell what will follow?

Sticks and Stones

UNCLE MEYER TUSSLED with two young hoodlums who tried to rob his store. You might think that at sixty-five he would be more concerned about life and limb than about his store, but for Meyer the store is his life. At one time it was the only grocery in the neighborhood. Now it is surrounded by supermarkets, and most of the customers are the old-timers who shop there out of loyalty, or because Uncle Meyer still extends credit to those who don't have ready cash. More than anything, the store still exists because of Meyer's obstinate will.

The store is open six days a week, from early morning till night, and on market days Meyer is up by four in the morning so that he can pick out his own produce. He personally handles the packing and unpacking of heavy boxes and tosses fifty-pound sacks of potatoes over his shoulder. He has remained a slender, wiry man with surprising strength and agility. He likes to bowl on Tuesday evenings and in his younger days he was a track star at New Utrecht High School and a pretty good left-handed handball player.

Meyer's corner grocery has been robbed several times, but the last episode was the most distressing. The previous robberies were done at night, by stealth, when the store was closed. A window was smashed, a door broken, the wires to the alarm cut, and the store left in a shambles. Once, out of sheer perversity, the burglars unplugged the freezers so that when Meyer opened the store on Monday morning, the floors were soaked and the food was spoiled. Meyer was disgusted.

"Those aren't people. They're animals. They ought to be treated like animals."

Meyer could accept the eventuality that bands of "animals" would periodically break into his store and leave him to absorb the losses and clean up the mess afterward. At least these robbers played by some implicit set of rules: They struck at night, in darkness, when he wasn't there to prevent it.

The last robbery was different, and that is why it was so disturbing. The two hoodlums weren't content to steal his goods; they tried to steal his pride as well. They arrogantly came into the store in the middle of the afternoon, without even a pretense of stealth, during one of the frequent lacunae when no customers were present. They treated him with contempt, as though he were a weak old man. They didn't even bother to show weapons. They just snapped orders.

One of them pointed to the cash register and said, "OK, Pops, open it up and maybe we won't hurt you too bad."

His companion reached into the cooler and pulled out a pack of beer.

"Yeah, Pops, and put this on my tab. Send the bill to my accountant."

Insolence, condescension, disrespect. He was nothing to them. Meyer flew into a rage. He lunged at the startled pair and shoved and pushed them roughly out the door before they realized what had happened.

"Get out of my store! Who do you think you are pushing around? You are worse than animals."

They were startled into submission. They were out of the store and on the sidewalk when one of them finally took a swing at Meyer. He intercepted the punch and delivered one of his own to the thug's stomach, causing him to double over. Meyer turned to the second hoodlum to give him the same treatment but his foot got caught in a crack in the sidewalk. There was a snap, like the sound of a dry twig under a heavy foot. Meyer felt a stab of pain. He fell without being touched. He struggled to his feet and tried to strike out, but he went down again because of the pain. Now the two thugs, their courage returned, started to work Meyer over. That might have been the end of him but, miraculously, a passing car stopped and a young man, a total stranger, jumped to his aid. He chased the assailants away, helped Meyer to his feet, and drove him to the hospital.

It wasn't long before Meyer was back in his store, earlier than the doctor wanted him there, on crutches. His ankle was fractured and his face bruised. He cursed the concrete as much as he did his attackers.

"If I hadn't caught my foot, I'd have handled those punks myself. They treated me like a nobody. I'd like to get my hands on them again."

Eventually they got their due. When you live and work in the same place for more than forty years you get to know all kinds of people, including some who have an uncommon interest in maintaining decorum and in keeping the police out of the neighborhood. These acquaintances heard of Meyer's misadventure and the word went out. The store was not to be disturbed again. And the two young freelancers were to be taught a lesson in manners and in respect for their elders.

Meyer has recovered but an invisible scar remains. His body has healed, but his spirit was wounded. Ironically, the most painful blow was delivered not by the swaggering punks who wanted to destroy him, but by the stranger who came to his aid. Of course he saved Uncle Meyer's life. And of course it's a miracle these days that anyone would put himself in danger for someone he doesn't even know. But, as he jumped out of the car to defend Uncle Meyer, the young man, his champion, shouted at the punks: "Hey you two, let go of that old man."

"Old man!" That stung Uncle Meyer. That wound has been slow to heal.

Uncle Meyer's Pickle Barrel

AT NICOLOFF'S SHOE Repair in South Minneapolis I had one of those delightful and unexpected experiences that connect the present with a past that often seems too distant to have been real. Mr. Nicoloff, by the way, is no longer the proprietor of the shoe repair store he inherited from his father. He has passed on to his reward; he died with his boots on, working in the shop until his final days. I've lived in the neighborhood and traded with Nicoloff for almost twenty-five years. After his death, I had a brief flirtation with Fast Eddie's shoe shop in Dinkytown, near the university where I worked, but I eventually returned to Nicoloff's even though Mr. Nicoloff no longer ran the shop.

On my recent visit I had hardly bared the soles (and heels) of my very old brown shoes when an unfamiliar woman behind the counter asked me where in New York I was from. That startled me. I haven't lived in New York since 1954. As an undergraduate in speech pathology at Brooklyn College I had been required to take a course in "speech pedagogy" that was supposed to eradicate my Brooklyn accent. How could she know I was from New York? Besides, it was almost a year since the last visit from my mother and Aunt Esther, so I hadn't had my annual Brooklynese booster yet.

The woman at Nicoloff's spotted me in a minute because she, too, was a displaced New Yorker. I soon learned that we had gone to different high schools. David Geffen and Buddy Hackett had been students at New Utrecht, where I went. The lady at Nicoloff's claimed Barbra Streisand at her school, Erasmus Hall. It seemed a standoff though my personal opinion is that Hackett and Geffen trump Streisand. I had another card up my sleeve in this game of Brooklyn-upmanship, however. I had delivered groceries to the home of the popular singer Vic Damone, and had often talked with his sister, Theresa.

Now she was skeptical. "I thought you lived in Bensonhurst."

"Yes," I said, "but my Uncle Meyer owned the grocery store on the corner of Cropsy and Bay 22nd, and I worked as a delivery boy when I was a teenager."

"I know that store," she said. "I used to shop there."

"Give me a sign," I told her. "Tell me a secret word or reveal some information that only someone familiar with the store could know."

She thought for a moment and then said, "The pickle barrel. There was an old-fashioned wooden pickle barrel just to the left as you entered the store. It was filled with sour pickles and green tomatoes and I'd reach in and get my own pickle, the brine running down my fingers, for a nickel—or a dime."

"It depended whether it was sour or half sour," I said, quite excited now. It had to be true. She was a stranger, but part of my past. We spent the next half hour reminiscing, ranging widely, talking about how we had gotten to Minnesota, our families, who was left in Brooklyn, what remained of our former attachments.

It was a thrilling half hour. I left there aglow, remembering and re-experiencing those earlier years. I didn't see her again. She was only filling in for the owner that day and was never there when I returned. Not long afterward the shop closed and reopened as an automobile-parts store. Anyway, it wouldn't be the same on another occasion. I'd be too busy, or too preoccupied for the magic of nostalgia to work in quite the same way. But it was wonderful for those moments to bring Uncle Meyer's grocery store to South Minneapolis, and I could almost taste the sour pickle, my teeth breaking through the resistant outer skin, then the juice flooding my mouth as the pickle exploded into mouth-watering taste. Marvelous! They don't make 'em that way anymore, and you certainly won't find them on the grocery shelf.

My Brief Career as a
Medical Student

ANY THOUGHTS I HAD about going to medical school and becoming a doctor ended very early in my college career—during my first semester at Brooklyn College, in an introductory biology course.

One of the first assignments in the lab section of that course was to dissect a frog. We students sat at a long table on which were a number of large bell jars. Inside each jar was a live specimen—in other words, a frog. My live specimen was active and intelligent. It hopped from one side of the jar to the other and pressed its face against the surface, its big, bulgy eyes staring at me. I felt that it liked and trusted me, and I formed a bond with it.

Immediately on the table in front of me was another, less-fortunate, specimen, a sister or a cousin to the one in the jar. The table specimen was fastened to a board with pins, and it was already a goner. It had been "pithed" by the instructor with a long needle. That was the one I was supposed to dissect. The student next to me was a frail girl, surely not cut out for this kind of work, I thought, but she had her sleeves rolled up and insisted that she could do her own pithing. She plunged right into her frog, wielding the scalpel with cheerful enthusiasm. On the other side of me was a big, strapping, muscular fellow. He also had his sleeves rolled up, and had a pack of Camel cigarettes in his breast pocket. He picked up the scalpel, bent over his frog, raised his scalpel—and passed out.

I surveyed the scene. My female partner was already doing a heart transplant and my macho partner with the muscular arms was sitting quietly in a corner, dreaming of a peaceful meadow somewhere. That left me, and I hadn't even begun the assignment.

I picked up the sharp, glittering scalpel, mentally drew a line where I would make the first cut, looked in the lab manual to be sure it was right, and turned toward my specimen. I might have been all right, but I chanced to look up at the bell jar and saw my victim's cousin or sister pressed against the side of the jar, staring at me with a soulful look that reminded me of an aunt on my father's side of whom I had always been fond.

I could not make that first cut. My enthusiastic partner had already neatly isolated all the organs and vessels in her frog and was waiting for the instructor to approve. She was bored and disdainful that I had made no progress.

"Barbara," I said, "I can't seem to get the hang of this. Could you help me out?"

She pushed me out of the way and assumed command, humming to herself with enthusiasm. She didn't even look up when I slunk away from the table and out of the room, careful not to look at the specimen in the bell jar as I fled.

That was the end of my career as a medical student. I flunked the course. Next semester the macho fellow and I took the course again, but we pretended not to recognize each other.

A Suit with Two
Pairs of Pants

I DON'T ENJOY shopping, especially for clothes. I am intimidated by the long racks (wracks?) of clothes and the mirrors that trap me into staring at the blemishes on my skin and the bulges in my frame. To my mind, if you want encounter therapy, go look in one of those mirrors.

Imagine this scene in an expensive men's store. The salesman is trying to close out a sale. After having shown me a half dozen jackets, he turns to my wife and finally exclaims:

"This is the one. This jacket is a perfect fit. It's made for him."

Eileen, my wife, is not persuaded. "It droops in the shoulders," she says.

The salesman is getting irritated. "It doesn't droop, lady. He droops."

He takes another garment from the rack and I have a glimmer of hope that maybe this will be the one perfect jacket made for my imperfect and undeserving body. He says to my wife, "If this doesn't satisfy you, nothing will. It makes him look like a million."

Eileen is not intimidated. "Look at that color. It's not his color."

The salesman is now indignant. Not only his garments, but his taste has been impugned. "Where you been, Missus? That's the color they're all wearing. It's the fashion."

"Humph! That color makes him look green!"

It's true. By then I do look green. I want out of there, desperately. I don't care about color, about style, even about size. Anything is fine with me. Double-breasted or no-breasted; solid color or polka dots. All I can think of is escape, freedom.

I finally speak up, earnestly, enthusiastically. "It's great," I say. "Beautiful. Just what I would have picked for myself. Let's buy it quickly before someone else snatches it from us."

When I get it home and try it on in privacy, I don't like it. My wife was right. The jacket doesn't fit properly in the shoulders and the color makes me look green. But I'm not going back to that store. It hangs in the closet until, mercifully, it goes out of style and I can contribute it to Goodwill.

Until I was sixteen I rarely bought clothes in a store. My grandfather was a tailor and from the time I was old enough to wear trousers he turned out every stitch himself. The pretext was always the same. Some Sunday morning he would be at our apartment and would stare at me in disbelief.

"Is it possible?" he would say. "I think you've been growing again. This is getting serious. I better check."

Then he would pull out his ever-present tape measure, make a few rapid passes around my waist and shoulders, and murmur knowingly. A week later he would reappear with a mysterious parcel under his arm which, to the amazement of all, would turn out to be an exquisitely tailored new pair of trousers and a matching jacket, both of which fit perfectly. It was only when my grandfather died that I was cast adrift in the world of merchant clothiers.

I remember one incident especially well, although it happened years ago, just before I was married. Eileen decided that it was time for me to replace the old gray cloth coat I'd been wearing since we had been going together. Before I knew what was happening, I was being propelled by Eileen and my future in-laws down the labyrinthine streets of New York's East Side, where the real bargains were to be found. Salesmen stood beckoning seductively at the entrance of clothing stores like the barkers at the topless bars in New Orleans. People were everywhere, crowding, jostling, all in pursuit of the ultimate bargain—the suit with two pairs of pants and a one-pair price.

We entered a store with a familiar name: Abe Stark's Fine Clothing. Abe Stark was a Brooklyn councilman who owned clothing stores. An enthusiastic salesman pulled overcoat after overcoat from the bulging racks, but none was quite right. Too short, too long, too tailored, too expensive. Always too something. The salesman became agitated as he saw his sale slipping away. Suddenly a gleam of inspiration lit his face. He said:

"I can see you're a smart young man. I'll bet you're in college. Am I right?"

"Yes, I'm in college."

"Of course. I could tell immediately that you're a smart young man. You're in college, and you plan to go to medical school. Right?" He flashed a beaming smile.

"Well, actually, no, I intend…"

He didn't wait for me to finish. He was now dripping with warmth and solicitude. He pointed to the sign in the store window. "Do you know whose store this is? This store belongs to Councilman Abe Stark. And do you know what it means to get a good word from Abe Stark when you apply to medical school? I mean, if Abe Stark wants a bright young fellow to get into medical school—a well-dressed young fellow— that person gets in, and that's that. Now, I'm not promising anything, but it certainly couldn't hurt if I whispered a few words in Abe's ear."

He looked at me knowingly, a look that was pregnant with meaning and promise. The road from Abe Stark's clothing store led directly to medical school, with a terrific bargain on a beautiful coat along the way.

I'd had as much as I could endure. I blurted out to Eileen, "Please, let's leave. No coats, no medical school. My old coat is fine. Let's just go home."

The salesman stared in disgust as I headed for the door. He shouted after me, "All right, but you just blew your chance for medical school."

OF COURSE, THIS is an old memory. I never did get into medical school, but I hadn't intended to. I still dislike shopping, but sometimes it's unavoidable. Just recently I decided to buy a new pair of trousers to go with my rust-colored jacket, the one I got about seven years ago. I saw an ad for one of the exclusive men's stores on Marquette Avenue, in Minneapolis. They were having a sale. This store was quiet, dignified, proper. The salesman was cool and attentive, not excessively friendly. For a moment he looked familiar, but no. It's just my mind playing tricks on me.

"I'd like to buy a pair of pants to match this jacket," I said.

The salesman stared at the jacket in a way that made my confidence ebb. After all, this was a clothing store, that man was a clothing salesman, cut from the same cloth, so to speak, as that other from my past. He gave me an appraising glance and steered me to a section with marked-down trousers. He selected a pair for me.

I took the pants from him and said, more meekly than I intended, "These are nice. How much are they?"

That was the giveaway. If I had to ask, I didn't belong. When he told me the sales price, I gasped audibly. I had never spent that much for a suit. In a feeble attempt at humor, I said, "I hope that includes the suspender buttons."

Without the trace of a smile he answered icily, "They aren't wearing these with suspenders."

It couldn't be, but it was happening once more, a thousand miles from the East Side. I might have been standing in Abe Stark's again. Suddenly, I understood. The revenge of a thwarted clothing salesman is not bounded by time or space. I had to escape. I stuttered something about coming back with my wife, and pushed past the salesman toward the door. As I left he called after me, patronizingly.

"I wouldn't waste any money matching up a pair of pants with that jacket. That jacket, it's got *narrow lapels*!"

It did. It did. And my color was green. But I was out of there. Free and safe once more.

Except for one thing. I shudder to think about it. My Uncle Meyer and Aunt Ann are having their sixty-fifth anniversary in a few months and there's going to be a big party in New York. Of course I'm going. The whole family is going to be there. Eileen has already bought herself a new outfit. Nice. Not too dressy. Just right.

That's wonderful, no? Except that Eileen says she's not going with me unless I buy a new suit. Maybe this time I'll go to Belleson's. I've heard that the salesmen there all have degrees in clinical psychology or social work.

The House I Lived In

IN 2005 MY WIFE and I moved into a condominium in Edina, a genteel suburb of Minneapolis. Our condominium complex is small—only sixteen units rather than one of those high-rise mega-structures that I find so repellent—and our unit is quite spacious. I have a very comfortable office where I was able to arrange the furniture precisely as it was in our old house. Our kitchen is larger than in our former home and the living room and dining areas are more than adequate. We found room for our piano, though no one plays it, and all of our furniture looks quite proper in these new "digs." We live on the first floor, very close to a side entrance and an elevator if we need it to get to the heated garage. We don't have to fuss about gardening or snow removal. These are the reasons we moved. But though we live in close proximity to fifteen other families, there is little mingling except for occasional encounters at the mail boxes or the garage. People here respect each other's privacy. There are no pets (by condominium rule), and no children except for the occasional visit of a grandchild. Many of the owners are here for only half the year, spending the winter months in warmer climes. It is a perfect place for a quiet life. Perhaps that's why I'm not really at home here. What I miss is a *neighborhood*, a place where people don't mind their own business, where the kids next door feel free to hide behind your shed when playing hide-and-seek, where someone down the block knocks on your door to ask whether you know that your child is perched precariously on the roof, where you might mysteriously find your walk shoveled in winter, and where neighbor kids show up in costumes on Halloween and you have to make believe you don't know who they are.

In the first ten years of our marriage we lived at eleven different addresses in four different states until we settled into our home
in South Minneapolis and planted a tree and ourselves. Our first
two years in Minneapolis, from 1961 to 1963, we rented an upstairs
apartment on Penn Avenue, in the North Side neighborhood of Minneapolis that had once been the site of a thriving Jewish culture. As
the neighborhood declined and our landlords, who lived below us,
became increasingly annoyed at the sounds of David and Karen racing along the uncarpeted floors above them, it became apparent that
it was finally time for this Brooklyn boy to succumb, however reluctantly, to the American dream.

Eileen found a house within our budget right down from the
Washburn water tower in a neighborhood of wandering streets,
called Tangletown. Long after we had moved in, Eileen told me that
it had been advertised as a "handyman's delight." The house was nes-
tled in the intersection of two streets that ran a short distance and
then vanished. Gladstone Avenue began at Fiftieth Street and ended
two blocks south, at Fifty-Second Street. Longview Terrace began at
Gladstone Avenue and ran for only one block, ending at the water
tower hill, one of the highest spots in Minneapolis. The Olsons had
bought the house from their parents, and it had been owned by only
one family before them, the St. Maries. Rooting around in the attic, I
discovered an envelope addressed to St. Marie dated 1925. The house
had been built in 1922. It was on two levels and had a finished basement. The front entrance could be approached either from Gladstone
Avenue or from Longview Terrace. There was also a door from the
kitchen leading to the back yard and still another door in the basement that led to the garage and then to Longview Terrace. Imagine,
three separate entrances!

The house seemed huge. Three floors. There should have been
at least three families living in it. David and Karen each had a bedroom with a closet, windows, and room for dressers and toys. The
windows in the master bedroom (who was this Master?) looked out
on either Longview Terrace or Gladstone Avenue. Our bedroom was
high up, near the treetops. In Brooklyn I shared a tiny bedroom with

my brother who is six years younger than I am: two beds and a small dresser. We couldn't stand up at the same time.

Our new home had a laundry chute. There was an opening to the chute in the upstairs bathroom and another in the kitchen. Oh, the excitement of opening the little door in the bathroom and dropping a truck, a doll, or some other object from the top floor and then racing to the basement to see it resting at the bottom of the chute; or climbing onto the kitchen sink to watch as a missile launched by your sister above careened down on the way to the basement. Our children and later our grandchildren found this an endlessly enjoyable game. We also discovered that many things could become lodged in the chute. Sometimes a week's worth of soiled clothes would disappear only to be found jammed in the chute between the upper and lower doors. That led to skill and ingenuity as we fashioned devices to free up the malodorous articles of clothing. What a satisfying sound it was when a clump of unsorted laundry finally broke free and plummeted down the chute on its way to the washing machine.

Trees. Our neighborhood's twisting and undulating streets were graced with trees, mostly elm. In fact, one of the streets is named Elm Street. Our corner enjoyed an especially magnificent specimen, easily eighty to one hundred years old. It provided a canopy of shade for numerous houses in its embrace, including ours. When the Dutch elm disease began to infect the trees in the city, we were among the first to treat the tree, and continued to do so for several years. The tree was huge, and standing in front of it I was dwarfed and awed. As the disease spread more and more rapidly throughout the cities, we feared for the welfare of our tree. "When that tree goes," we said, "we go too." One day we saw the ominous red circle drawn around the trunk indicating it was slated for destruction. We pleaded with the city to spare it but when we were shown a slice of the infested bark we knew it was hopeless. The ground shook and tears were shed when the workmen felled that mighty tree over the course of an entire day. And, indeed, not long afterward we moved to our current suburban home after forty-two years in the shade of that beautiful tree.

There is still another tree story. I was on sabbatical in California when a new owner moved into the house directly across the street from us, where the Glennons had lived. When I returned from sabbatical all of the trees along the side of his house and in his backyard were gone. I learned that shortly after he and his wife bought this new home, she left him. He took out his fury on the trees, and now the sole survivor was a beautiful mountain ash in his front yard. Every fall its branches were laden with clusters of bright orange berries.

I was working in the second floor bedroom that I had converted into my office. Glancing out of the window I could see the new owner on his front lawn, walking around and around the ash tree. He was a youngish fellow although practically bald. Now that he had measured the tree, he began darting up and down a ladder, a chain saw in his hand. Each time he climbed up, *zzzzzzzp* went the saw and crash came one of the limbs. He threw a rope to the top and snared a limb. Then he tied the end of the rope to a railing in front of his house. He scampered up the ladder, sawed through the limb, scampered down the ladder and tugged at the rope until the limb fell free.

He removed his cap and I could see the excited beads of sweat on his forehead. He stared upward for a moment, moved the ladder, tossed the rope again, and cut off another limb, a handsome arching branch. Little by little the limbs, branches, and twigs fell into piles. Then he attacked the trunk. He cut the trunk and branches into logs and tossed them against the side of the house. He began to dig at the roots. He was wearing a headband now and heavy gloves. He slashed at the roots, but they were stubborn. They would require another day. He took down the ladder and disappeared into his front doorway. I had just witnessed a cruel and violent assault. A day or two later I saw that he had smoothed the ground where the tree had stood and had planted flowers.

It wasn't long before he disappeared and a new family moved in. They took out the flower bed—and planted a tree.

A YEAR OR TWO after we had moved into our Gladstone Avenue home we planted a tree in our backyard. For Eileen and me, big-city

New Yorkers, planting a tree was romantic and exciting. (Years later we had that experience again when we planted trees in Israel.) The young Bachman's salesman understood how special this was for us. He helped us choose: a green mountain ash. After his workday he showed up in our backyard with the tree, just a tiny slip of a thing, and guided us to the proper spot, showed us how to dig the hole to the right depth, how to place the tree in the hole. It was drizzling and we took that as a sign of heavenly approval. Time after time I tested the girth of my growing tree as I passed it on the way in and out of our back door, until I could no longer enfold it because it had grown so wide. When we moved it was as though I had left a beloved household pet behind, but I was comforted with the knowledge that we had planted a tree, it had grown and thrived, and was bringing pleasure to another family.

Bathroom chronicle. Our second-floor bathroom had a tub and a separate shower stall. Of course there was no such thing in my Brooklyn home. Back in Brooklyn, my father once was taking a shower and Mollie Tannenbaum walked into our apartment (door unlocked), pushed open the bathroom door (unlocked), and loudly warned my dad, "Abe, don't open the shower curtain. I need to go and I don't want to walk all the way up." It now seems remarkable that the four of us in my family, plus an occasional visit from Mrs. Tannenbaum, all got by with one bathroom.

On Gladstone Avenue we had our full second-floor bathroom and a rather dingy affair in the basement (cellar, my mother called it), with just a stool and tiny sink. Getting at the shower in the morning was a challenge with three children lined up. Karen took to waking at the break of dawn to avoid the rush. The basement bathroom was used only for emergencies. One morning I heard loud screams from that area and rushed to see David standing on the toilet-seat cover. "There's an animal in there," he sputtered. I gingerly lifted the toilet-seat cover a crack, and there, head above the water, was a rat! I encouraged it back into the pipes and the sewer from whence it had decided to visit us.

Off the Wall. In 1990, we decorated our second-floor bathroom. To our surprise, when we removed the old wallpaper we discovered that the walls were covered with inscriptions. We had forgotten that the last time we papered the room, in 1975, we had asked the children to write a message on the bare walls before we covered them, a kind of time capsule for the next owners who would surely remove the wallpaper at some point and might be curious about the people who had lived there before them. We didn't anticipate that the first persons to read the inscriptions would be us. Fifteen years had elapsed and our children were all gone by then. The messages were not always clear. Some of the script came off with the wallpaper. I photographed the wall and transcribed what I could. As usual, Karen, the writer in our family, wrote the most: "It's too bad all this empty writing space must be covered with wallpaper. My name is Karen Siegel. I am the daughter of Gerald and Eileen Siegel. I am fourteen years old (born 1961). I love to write songs, stories, poems, anything! I am Jewish. Religion is an important source of identity for me. English and music are my favorite subjects at school…I hope whoever you are that is reading this that now you will understand that I am, in a sense, writing to you, and not to this wall. I am telling you things which I think you might want to know about me, about all of us. Perhaps when you have uncovered this you will leave something of yourself as well for the next people who come to live here. Take care of it. Karen."

David, always a list maker, identified all of our neighbors. On Longview Terrace: Raij, Kortright, Wilson, Efron, O'Brien, Fosse, Coskran, Sarat. On Gladstone: Farrell, Le Moyne, Burk, Mrs. Frommelt, Lecy, Waldfogel, Mrs. Welslager, Rasor, Davis, Malcolm, Bergstrom. He also gave a bit of personal history and ended with, "And I was here."

Josh drew a flower with an inscription on each of the leaves and indicated he was eight years old. He also wrote a poem: "Hey Wall!/ Roses are blue/And Violets are red/If you believe this/Examine your head."

And I added, "This wall/Will fall/And that'll/Be all." We didn't find the inscription Eileen had written.

Some Neighbors. Over the four-plus decades we lived in Tangletown, every house changed owners at least once, some many times, except for the indomitable Sarats who live up the block in the shadow of the water tower. Ginny's mother lived to 104 and it seems that Ginny and her husband, Sam, plan to challenge that record. They are amazingly fit, walking long distances every day. Their car license plates read, "L'Chaim"—to life.

Our closest neighbors were the Farrells. Effie loved to read. Willard screened in a patio for her at the back of their house and throughout the summer she would be there, a book in hand, except when she was preparing iced tea and lunch for Willard or scolding him for undertaking too difficult a job. Willard was a tall, strapping man. He did everything himself, much to Effie's dismay. He painted the outside of his house, climbed the cottonwood tree in his backyard to trim the branches, and was often on the roof of his house cleaning gutters or breaking an ice dam. Broken things that I put out for the garbage would appear, repaired, in his backyard. If Willard saw me working on a project in our backyard, he would climb over the fence to see whether he could "lend a hand," which usually meant taking over. One day he saw me struggling to remove a heavy metal post from the middle of our backyard that had been used to attach a laundry line. I dug and pushed and wiggled the post, but could not get it out of the ground. Will appeared with a jack from his car and slowly teased the post out of the ground, trailing a large clump of concrete. When Willard became ill, I shoveled his walk while the service I had hired shoveled mine. It would have embarrassed Will to have a paid stranger do his chores. When the Farrells moved, the Laubers took their place. Before they moved in, Mrs. Farrell whispered, "She's going to have a baby." She was right. Eleven months later Peyton was born.

Patty Daniels was married to a radio celebrity. They lived across the street on Gladstone Avenue. Patty ran a modeling agency and beautiful women trekked in and out of her home, especially on weekends. That's when several of us contrived to find some outdoor activity that kept us in sight of the front door. I also had a good view from our bedroom window. The Malcolms, an elderly couple, lived right next to them and poor Mr. Malcolm had to endure the sight of Patty and her entourage sunbathing in her backyard. He was stoic. I never heard him complain.

Irene and Bob Kortright were across the alley from us and became close friends. Irene was especially kind to our youngest son, Josh, and he was often at her house eating cookies and ice cream. When Irene's father died, her elderly mother, Babcha, came to live with them. I was to be in Boston for a conference and volunteered to escort Babcha to Minneapolis. She spoke little English and I no Polish. It was her first airline trip. She was a woman of considerable girth and not very mobile. I wondered what I would do if she needed to go to the bathroom during the long trip, but the problem never arose. Once she was ensconced in her second-floor bedroom on Longview Terrace, Babcha never left the house except for medical visits and once to see a traveling troupe of Polish dancers. Most of the time she sat in her upstairs room, peering out the window, taking in neighborhood comings and goings, much like Mrs. Reiff in my Brooklyn home.

Kay and Gene O'Brien lived a few houses up toward the water tower. They were the second generation in their house, and I suspect it was painful for them when it did not pass to any of their children. Gene was a bluff, loud-talking Irishman, a lawyer. One afternoon Gene rang our doorbell, flustered and agitated, to tell us our daughter had climbed out of her bedroom window and was sitting on the lower roof, dangling her feet over the ledge. When Eileen had to take a trip to New York because of a family emergency, Kay invited me for dinner. Their son Denny was there and we discovered we both played handball. Before the evening ended, Denny, quite a few years my junior, invited me to join him that very night on the courts at the Minneapolis Athletic Club. I doubt that Denny knew it, but only a few decades ago this facility had been closed to Jews. The O'Briens moved. I heard that Gene had died. Several years later Eileen and I were at an open house for our friends the Wolks on James Avenue, and Kay and her new husband arrived. They lived across the street. Kay greeted us both warmly.

American Idyll? We never had a serious argument with any of our neighbors, but it would be false to imply there were never disagreeable incidents among Tangletown residents. Across the street from us two families shared a common driveway, and they became locked in a dispute over a property line. It was serious enough that when one of them shoveled his half of the driveway, he would pile the snow on the other half. Peggy, who had an asthmatic child, became incensed when Burke sprayed a chemical on the backyard lawn. They haven't spoken since.

Mrs. Farrell, of whom we were very fond—and she of us—invariably attached the word "rich" any time she used the word "Jew." Kay, who generously invited me to dinner when Eileen was away, came back from a church trip to Israel, furious at what she had been told about the mistreatment of Christian religious sites by the Israelis, a charge I knew to be untrue.

Stan offered to order a yard of dirt that we could share to repair our lawns. His home was up toward the water tower. When the dirt arrived, he had all of it delivered in front of his house. He offered me a shovel and wheelbarrow, but no help. I filled the wheelbarrow, wheeled it down to our backyard, dumped the load, wheeled up the hill again to the pile of dirt, refilled the wheelbarrow, and repeated this cycle over and over while he observed from his front window. It started to rain and he helpfully opened his window to suggest I work faster because the dirt became heavier when wet.

We had a snow-removal service. During one especially bad winter they were out shoveling our sidewalks and driveway at two o'clock in the morning. Steve, who lived across Gladstone Avenue, called to complain about the noise. To me, that was not noise. The sound of shovels scraping against concrete was music! People have different tastes in music.

It was inevitable that over so long a time span there would be losses. Two young fathers died, one in a tragic hunting incident, the other of cancer. Several marriages died, too. Stan, with whom I shared the dirt, left his wife after many years of marriage, and she eventually sold the house. Older residents sought out assisted-living facilities as they became infirm. Always, they were replaced by families who loved the neighborhood, laid claim to the water tower, mourned the old trees and planted new ones.

On the Street. Our children played on the streets. In winter they slid down the steep incline on our front lawn, and when they were older, down the water-tower hill all the way to the corner of Gladstone and Longview. In warm weather they swarmed around the water tower or played kickball and other games in the street, much as we had in Brooklyn. The neighborhood was filled with children: one family alone had twelve, playmates enough for any age. Our backyard was a gathering place for soccer and for our annual June fourteenth celebration of Flag Day and my birthday. Minnehaha Creek was only a few blocks away, and the newly renovated library could be reached readily by bike. On the Fourth of July a fire truck parked on our corner before escorting the children on bikes, trikes, and strollers decorated red, white, and blue to a picnic along the creek. Children poured out of their homes on Halloween and brought back bags of candy. Occasionally a neighbor would scream at a car that was driving recklessly through the neighborhood. As the years passed, there were also changes in the pulse of activity. Out of concern and caution that some sick person would attempt to harm them, parents began to prohibit their children from playing in the streets or near the water tower. Instead the children had "play dates." This felt like a loss.

Renovations. We hired professionals for big jobs. Irv "Ole" Swanson built a large shed for us in the backyard. First he had to put down a cement slab. The cement was delivered in a truck with a rotating drum. Ole framed the space where the cement was to be poured and the truck operator, a huge man, emptied the cement load by load into a wheelbarrow that I was supposed to get to Ole in a hurry. The cement man looked on with glee as I staggered all over the backyard with the wheelbarrow, unable to keep it straight and balanced. In the end, Ole handled the wheelbarrow as well as putting in the slab. The cement truck operator didn't stir himself to help. Instead, he casually dumped the remaining cement in a heap at the edge of our backyard and took off, leaving Ole to do something with the mound of hardening cement. Ole quickly fashioned a set of steps from the alleyway into our backyard. He also replaced all of the kitchen cabinets and renovated our basement. It was a joy to watch him at work.

After the children were gone and there were only the two of us, we hired our neighbor Richard Haskins to add a bathroom on the first floor so that, like Molly Tannenbaum, we didn't need to climb stairs to the toilet. He also renovated our basement bathroom, even adding a shower. We created a rock garden on the south bank where it was impossible to grow grass, hauling rocks all the way from the North Shore of Minnesota and anywhere else we could find them. Once we slid off the road in pursuit of a very promising boulder. We landscaped, swapped out the old, heavy wooden storms and screens for more modern and less-efficient aluminum, had floors sanded to reveal the beautiful wood in some rooms, and had carpet replaced in others. Our relatives came to visit us in this strange new place that wasn't a stop on the New York subway system, my mother and Aunt Esther every Passover for thirty years. We hosted hundreds of dinners and numerous seders for our family and friends, opened our home to my university students, had innumerable birthday parties for our children, and had a shivah minyan when Eileen's brother Julius died and then, most painful of all, when our daughter Karen died in 2001.We lived fully in the house, from the attic to the basement. Our children and grandchildren inserted themselves into and rubbed against every inch. Our family lived hard in that house, and I think it approved, even if Eileen and I didn't always.

During our forty-two years at 5050 Gladstone Avenue I painted or wallpapered almost all of the rooms, put up shelves, laid carpet, changed light fixtures and switches, and painted the exterior trim of the house while clinging precariously to a high ladder. I did none of this cheerfully. I attacked each task with dread, but every job made the house a little more mine. I had my foot- and handprints all over it.

Eileen had been suggesting for some time that we should consider moving, and she looked at some properties but they were either too small, too far from familiar areas in South Minneapolis, or seemed not to offer much advantage over our Gladstone home, so we stayed put. I was glad. But it became too hard to maintain the house and to manage the stairs between the bedrooms, kitchen, and basement laundry room. It was time. We put our house up for sale just as the housing market was beginning to decline. We were lucky. Two maintenance workers for Northwest Airlines were starting a business buying old homes to refurbish and then sell at a profit. We accepted their bid and began the difficult process of saying goodbye to our neighbors and our home. The airline mechanics sold the house to a young couple with small children.

I occasionally drive through the neighborhood. The doors and windows have been replaced. The shed that Ole constructed is gone. The rock garden is gone. The French doors from the dining room that led to nothing now open to a patio facing Gladstone Avenue. There is a swing set in the backyard. The cycle is repeating. The Laubers invited us to a party at their house along with lots of our old neighbors and we met the new family who now live in 5050 Gladstone Avenue. We didn't get to visit very much, but they seemed like nice folks. I gave them a copy of the "Off the Wall" comments our children had written on the bathroom walls so many years ago.

The time capsule is finally in the right hands.

Courage

MY FATHER WAS wracked by fantasies that were, on the face of it, incredible, absurd, even pretentious. He imagined that he had committed robberies, burglaries, crimes of violence—acts that he couldn't possibly have done. Somewhere in the family genetic history or in his personal history, these fantasies had taken root and they plagued him throughout his adult life though I only learned of them late, when I was on the threshold of becoming an adult myself.

I have scant memories of my father's parents. Grandfather Joseph Siegel died when I was only a few months old, and Grandmother Celia when I was five. A few years ago my cousin Joseph, whom I'd not seen or spoken to in decades, asked if I would chip in to provide perpetual care for our grandfather's grave. I made my contribution for a grandfather I never knew, and then wondered what had happened to my grandmother. Cousin Joseph was no help. His preoccupations ended with his namesake. None of the surviving family members knows where she is buried. My father never spoke of his childhood or his parents and it didn't occur to me to be curious about them. It was Grandpa and Grandma Needleman, my mother's parents, who were a constant and important presence in my childhood.

From fragments of family history given me by my cousin Ruthie, I learned that Grandfather Siegel came from Vilna, Poland, in 1862 and died in New York in 1932, the year of my birth, having reached the biblical span of seventy. Celia Levy Siegel was born around 1860 in Lida, Poland, and died in 1937. They had nine or perhaps ten children. At least one of my father's brothers is known to have died as a child in Europe, and so they must have married there. Over the years I heard variously that my grandfather owned a grocery store, a candy store, worked as an orderly in a hospital, or in a foundry. They couldn't have been very well off. My mother and father were married in New York in 1930. Joseph and Celia were still alive, and so I presume they attended the wedding, but among my mother's trove of photographs there were no wedding pictures. Nothing in this sparse history explains my father's suffering.

My father's obsessions with guilt were all the more incredible because he was incapable of any dishonesty. If he found a dollar on the street, he couldn't keep it. If he failed to pay his dime on the trolley car, he would mail it in. When filing income tax he would gladly send in more money than required.

Among his fractious siblings, he was the peacemaker. The brothers and sisters were often angry and would not speak to each other. He was the dumpster for their ill will.

"Abe, your brother Harry is no good."

"Sadie, he is your brother too."

"Not since he cheated my Herman in the business, he isn't. I don't want him for a brother. And why are you sticking up for him?"

"I'm not sticking up for him. He's got plenty of troubles too, with that kid of his, and the emphysema, and the business on the rocks."

"He's a *gonif*, and he deserves whatever he gets, and you shouldn't be sticking up for him."

"Sadie, you should see him. He became ten years older in one year. He smokes like a chimney and he can't get a breath of air. He spends all of his time in that lousy loft, waiting for business."

"That's his reward for cheating my husband!"

It was Dad who made the cigarette run for Harry in the hospital after the business finally failed, who tried to persuade his sister that Harry was in a bad way, needed help. He performed similar service for his other brothers and sisters too.

Neighbors used him, and he welcomed it. He shopped at a discount drugstore and took orders from up and down the block.

"Mac, you need toothpaste? I'm going to the discount." And, in a hushed voice, "Trojans? Sure. What size? Only kidding."

"Bertha, you need something, I'm going to the discount? Razor blades for Sam? Anything else for Sam? OK, OK, I'm just asking."

My father had no mechanical skills. He didn't fix things. He ran errands. He was out of the house at six in the morning to get a loaf of bread and a half-dozen bagels so that Mac, who drove a cab at night, could sleep in a little later. He delivered the Yiddish newspaper to Mrs. Resnick's door. He answered the telephone at the candy store and raced to Louie to tell him he was wanted on the phone, and then hastened Louie along because time is money on the telephone, somebody's money. He told Jack that he had heard from Al that Evelyn was looking for him. When a death or a calamity occurred, he grieved with the grievers. Sunday mornings Izzy opened the candy store at four o'clock and Dad was there to help assemble the newspapers, though Izzy rewarded him only with a grunt: "What's the matter, she throw you out of the house? Hey, be careful there. The comics first, then the sports."

The Siegels were not greatly prized by my mother; her loyalties were circumscribed by her own blood relations. "Your father's family," she told me, "are a bunch of kooks."

"They're not just Dad's family. They're my family, too," I reminded her.

The Needlemans, my mother's tribe, were a disputatious group who thrived on disagreement, forceful commentary, table pounding, giving no quarter until the opponent slunk away. But they could not prevail over Dad. His fleetness was astonishing. He would find a way to agree with all points of view, standing first on one foot and then on the other. Communism is bad, but then again it has its good points. America should enter the war, but what business is it of ours? Children are wonderful, but see how ungrateful they are. Roosevelt is a great president, but look at the awful things he did. No one could stand up to him in an argument; he agreed so readily, it left his interlocutor breathless. There was no point of view so untenable that he couldn't find a germ of truth in it.

"What, you say the moon is made of green cheese? Hmm, I don't know, but now you mention it…oh, you said *cream cheese*? Well, now that you point it out, I've heard that, too." In frustration one of my uncles would say, "Abe, you are driving me crazy. First you say one thing and then just the opposite." And Dad would solemnly agree even with that.

I learned about my father's secret miseries when I was eighteen. I had completed my freshman year at Brooklyn College and needed a summer job. Dad worked at the Morgan Annex Post Office in New York. Stan, one of his co-workers, had a second job as a foreman of the shipping department of a dress-manufacturing company in the Garment District. Stan told my father he could get me a summer job in his department. I would be paid eighty cents an hour. Not bad for a college kid. The Puerto Ricans working there were supporting families on the same wage.

For eight hours a day throughout the summer I packed "half-size" dresses into cardboard boxes, sealed the boxes with brown tape and string, and brought them to the next station where they were shipped to customers all over the world. Sometimes the dresses were sent to locations in Puerto Rico, and the packer next to me would surreptitiously write a message in Spanish on the inside of the carton, messages of longing, I presumed.

Stan wasn't always on the premises, but when he was he liked to hang out with us college kids. One noon, during our lunch break, he regaled us with a story. He was a gruff character, but he was fascinating, too. He knew how to hold an audience.

"Siegel, come here. I want you to hear this," Stan called out from the anteroom to the shipping floor. He was sitting on a large crate, feet crossed under his bulky frame, a half-smoked cigar stuck in his mouth.

"You college kids think you know a lot, but I could teach you some things even though I never went to college. My kid's gonna go to college, but I could teach him some things too." He waited until he had everyone's attention.

"There was this guy who graduated from law school but he couldn't find a job during the Depression so he ended up in a factory, like me. He was educated but that didn't mean he was smart. Now get this—this educated jerk put the names of his relatives on the payroll and collected their pay envelopes every week. At the end of the year every one of them got a tax statement from a company they had never worked at. One of them went to the company to complain and it all unraveled. He never thought about that. He ended up in the slammer. You know the moral of this story? If you are going to be a crook, be smart about it."

He chewed on his cigar, lost in his own thoughts. Then he barked, "All right, back to work. This isn't the welfare department."

When my tax forms arrived the following winter, the forms showed that I had been on the payroll right through the end of the year. That made no sense. I had quit in August to return to college. I went back to the factory. Although shipping was on the same floor as the office and clerical pool, the two departments might have been in distant continents. Shipping clerks were treated with disdain. When a secretary or office worker had some business in our area, she was careful not to touch anything or anyone. Now I was going to enter the inner sanctum. First I stopped in the shipping department to see whether I might recognize anyone after five months. Stan was there.

"Where you going all dressed up?"

"Up front. They screwed up my tax forms, and I'm going to have the pleasure of pointing it out."

Stan turned white. "Listen, do me a favor, don't go in there. Let me take care of it. I can straighten it out for you."

"Hell, no. They messed up and I want them to admit it to my face."

I found the bookkeeper in her office, thrust my W-2 forms in front of her, and indignantly demanded an explanation. I was no longer a lowly shipping clerk. I had resumed my real identity as *Brooklyn College Superstudent.*

In a day or so I was summoned back and was met by one of the officers of the firm. He shook my hand cordially, invited me to sit in his office, asked after my college studies. Finally he told me that Stan had kept summer workers on the payroll throughout the year and collected our pay envelopes each week, much like the "educated jerk" in his cautionary tale. Stan had still another scam. He was being paid for working two jobs at the same time. A buddy at the post office punched his time-card while Stan was in the shipping department at the dress factory.

Stan was quietly fired from the factory, and just as quietly kept his job at the post office. He pleaded with us not to prosecute; he just needed money to send his kid to college. We didn't, we never could have.

My father was beside himself. He was sure that he was responsible for Stan's actions and had participated in a criminal act. They both should go to jail: Stan for his criminal acts, and my father for being an accomplice.

I was initiated into my father's illness. I learned that he had been under psychiatric care for decades—that he might be set off by a newspaper account of a robbery, a murder, or a burglary in some distant place. Reading about it, he became sure that he was the felon or the murderer, and he feared he would be discovered or, equally awful, that he would not be discovered and would have to live with his guilt. It didn't matter that it was physically impossible for him to have been at the scene of the crime. He *knew* he was guilty.

When these episodes came on him, he would walk the streets at night, become absorbed with his guilt, weep and plead with my mother for forgiveness, aware that it was all an awful dream but unable to shake its grip. These obsessions might last days or months, and then suddenly he was free but full of remorse for the anguish he had created for my mother. I had been oblivious to his suffering. Now I became a player in the family drama. There was a ritual we went through.

"Dad, you couldn't have been involved in that incident you read about. You were right here in the living room with Mom and me when it happened."

"Of course, you're right," my father would say. "But…"

"No! No! There is no 'but.' You weren't involved—couldn't have been."

We would go on like this until he finally, shamefully, acknowledged I was right, it was all in his mind. And then, relieved but not entirely, he might doze off in the living room chair. The next evening, after work, the scene would be replayed. My mother would absent herself. This was between Dad and me now. It was my job to play out the script as she had over the years.

As time went on he was plunged deeper and deeper into despair, until I could no longer reason with him. The routines we had established no longer worked.

"Pop, we told you. It wasn't your fault."

"That's not it. It's just too much. It's just too much for me. It's just too much."

I followed him as he walked to Kings County Hospital, wishing to escape, to commit himself to the psychiatric ward—but then, he couldn't push himself past the entrance, and so he returned with me in tow and fell exhausted into bed. Now the fear was pure, existential, no longer connected to any imagined crime, and all the more terrifying for that.

Eventually time assuaged what it would not heal. The agony abated. Routines were reestablished. He brought home his paycheck, delivered the newspaper to Mrs. Resnick, a loaf of bread to Mac, as before. He went to work every day but his step was slower and his sleep more fitful. He became preoccupied and silent.

My father's devoted service included his psychiatrist of many years. Every couple of weeks he visited Dr. Ciarello with a head full of troubles and a bag full of goodies. Dad knew Dr. Ciarello's favorite brand of razor blades, toothpaste, shaving cream, foot powder. I was well into my college career now—had taken courses in psychology. I visited Dr. Ciarello in his office.

"Your father is obsessive-compulsive," he told me.

"I've studied about that," I said, "but what have you done for him all of the years he has been your patient? And how can you accept gifts from him?"

He gave me a look that made me feel I was back in the shipping department.

"I keep him going. Doing things for me makes him feel useful. I get him through the days, year after year. He relies on me. What do you think would happen to him if I were not here to see and reassure him?"

I had no answer. I knew that Dad panicked when the doctor was on vacation or unavailable. The receptionist would try to refer him to someone else, but, no, it had to be Dr. Ciarello. I felt that the doctor was taking advantage of my father's neediness but I didn't dare say that. This was one of the anchors in his life; it could not be disturbed.

I turned twenty-one, graduated college, and was married, all within a one-week span. A year later I completed my MA degree at Brooklyn College and was accepted for doctoral study at the University of Iowa. It was a time for celebration. My parents were proud that I was pursuing an advanced degree, but also felt abandoned. My father was sure I was fleeing from him.

My brother Joel, six years younger than I, stayed behind and slipped into the slot I had vacated, talking with my father, reasoning with and reassuring him. The relationship was different, however. They did things together. My father became a leader in my brother's scout troop and accompanied him to sleep-over camp. I had not been in the scouts. They went to ballgames and on excursions together, my father leading groups of children. My parents gave Joel a car when he graduated from high school, and he took my father places. I didn't get my license until I had finished my doctoral studies at Iowa.

Joel graduated from college and also married. My mother went to work and brought extra money into the household. For the first time, they were not scraping for every dollar. They visited us in Iowa. Dad was uneasy in this new environment. I was being educated at a major university. This was hallowed ground where great minds reposed, men of brilliance and huge mental powers. He was awed. He responded to me as he did to people of status and authority. And I was impatient, preoccupied with my studies.

After thirty-eight years, he retired from the post office and took a civil-service test. He passed and now had a job in the city welfare department. This ought to have been a period of tranquility, but for my father the sense of well-being provoked feelings of unworthiness. He ruminated about the hardships he had inflicted on his family. He wrote notes to himself on scraps of paper describing his remorse, and hid them among his private belongings. We found them after he died.

He and my mother went on a real vacation, the first in years, to Miami Beach. It was marvelous that they could afford to go where so many of their friends had been before them. A trip to the "Holy

Land," they joked. Not long after they returned Dad had difficulty walking, was short of breath. He made two more trips. I was scheduled to give a talk at a professional conference in Washington, DC, an honor for me. Mom and Dad decided to attend. Afterward we did some sightseeing. Dad could not manage the steps to the Lincoln Memorial. In May our son Joshua was born in Minneapolis, and Mom and Dad came for the bris. Dad was the sandek; he held the baby during the circumcision ceremony.

He went back to work at the welfare department when they returned to New York. It was his custom to bring a sandwich and call my mother from a pay telephone during his lunch break. On December 1, 1966, a little more than six months after the visit to Minneapolis, Dad called home as usual and just as he connected he had a massive heart attack. He spoke no words. Sam Haroldson called me out of the class I was teaching at the University of Minnesota. I flew to New York and the next day my brother and I identified his body in the morgue. My mother never had the chance to say goodbye and only Joel and I saw the body before the interment. He was sixty-three years old.

Rabbi Silverman presided at the funeral. Not long before, he had presented my father with a watch in appreciation for Dad's services to the synagogue men's club. In his eulogy, the rabbi extolled my father's unselfishness, generosity, helpfulness, devotion to family and community, the usual virtues.

"And finally," the rabbi continued, "Abe Siegel was a man of personal courage."

That last sentence seemed odd, as though the rabbi had misplaced his notes. Maybe he had another funeral that day. Dad was a good guy, a *mensch*, but courageous?

"You are thinking," the rabbi continued, "that bravery is for warriors or heroes, not for simple souls. Courageous is the lion, not the mouse. But the lion roars and all flee from his path. Not so the tiny mouse. His little squeak is an invitation to potential disaster. He faces great danger each time he ventures from his hiding place to find food. So, I ask you, which is the more courageous, the great lion whom all fear, or the lowly mouse who fears all?"

Izzy leaned over to his wife, Rae. "You know, I think he's got something there."

Rae answered, above a whisper, "What's any of this got to do with Abe, stories of lions and mice?"

The rabbi, of course, heard and reddened, but he continued.

"Abe lived a life of private pain. And yet, except when the pain was overwhelming, he showed up for work, he extended himself for others, he performed g*emilut hasadim*—deeds of loving-kindness. That might not sound like much, but for Abe it meant day after day of fighting and struggling for his dignity. It took courage to remain good-natured and generous when he had so little hope for himself. He suffered guilt for crimes that he never committed. He bore gifts and messages, but never animosity or anger toward others. Like Job, he would not curse God."

Rae: "Finally, something to do with the Bible."

Izzie: "Shh. I'm listening."

"It never occurred to him—he would have denied it—but Abe lived a life of courage equal to the fears that haunted him. Despite his pain, he did not forgo his acts of service. These were simple deeds, but against the demons Abe had to cope with, they were also deeds of valor. He did not have the lion's roar...

"Oh no. Not back to lions and mice."

"Please, I'm trying to listen."

"...But he was, after all, a courageous man. May he find eternal peace and may his memory be for a blessing..."

As the rabbi spoke, in my mind I heard my own voice, touched with regret, and it almost drowned him out: "He was so proud of you. You could have honored him more, empathized with his suffering, acknowledged his love and sacrifices."

The rabbi concluded, "And let us say, 'Amen.'"

"Amen!" Friends, neighbors, and onlookers joined their voices to the rabbi's.

I, too, sounded an amen from deep within my grieving heart. "Amen. *Amen.*"